AN ARTIST'S HORIZONS

Sextant Sight, ZAVORAH. Watercolor, 1937, 73:14 ½″ x 21″.

Dwight Shepler

AN ARTIST'S HORIZONS

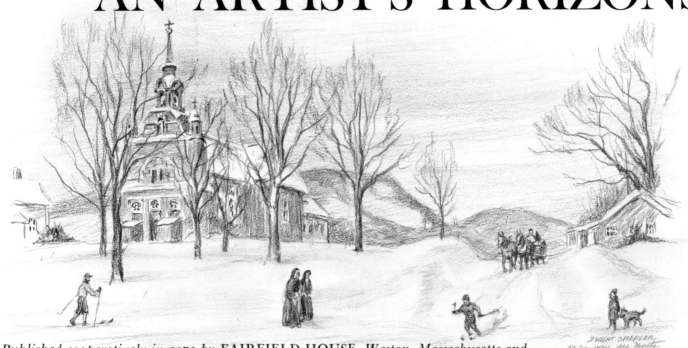

Published cooperatively in 1973 by FAIRFIELD HOUSE, *Weston, Massachusetts and*

BARRE PUBLISHERS, *Barre, Massachusetts*

Library of Congress Catalog Card Number: 72–95108
ISBN 8271–7254–0

To the memory of Alden P. Johnson, 1914-1972, erudite and
inspirational founding president of Barre Publishers,
who first planned this book

Contents

Illustrations

Photo credits: reproduction is almost entirely from originals. Certain negatives were supplied by George M. Cushing, Frank Kelley, Peter Juley, Howard J. Levitz, Everett Studios, Sibley Photo, and Peter Vose.

Acknowledgments

The author and limner of this first book is most appreciative of the generosity and enthusiasm of the owners of paintings, listed on the final page, who lent work for this book. The feat of locating many of these originals, spread far and wide over the years, was achieved largely through the definitive records compiled by my wife, Hennie, who also has been companion and helpful critic in the making of most of the pictures. The deadline of the manuscript was met by the typing assistance of daughter, Ann Albright, whose clear eye caught inconsistencies in the text.

The warp and woof was woven under the skilled direction of Ronald Johnson and Jon Beckmann of Barre Publishers. The latter's editorial perception in aligning diffuse ideas was of essential value. In 1971–72 I had worked with Harold Hugo, president of The Meriden Gravure Company, as editor of *A. Lassell Ripley, Paintings*, which was published by the Guild of Boston Artists in co-operation with Barre Publishers. *An Artist's Horizons* has been the recipient of his expertness and advice, and that of his staff. One is indeed fortunate to have his work printed by such a house, supreme in its field. The skills of Raymond M. Grimaila are evident in the design of this volume, while less obvious are his esoteric ones of co-ordinating color and black and white plates with the sequences of the text. To work with associates whose basic quest is excellence is the best part of the whole effort.

I am especially grateful for the "foreword" written by my blue-water sailing and publishing friend, Melville Grosvenor, whose name is better known to ten-out-of-ten people than that of the author.

Foreword

Our wakes first crossed at the onset of World War II. Dwight Shepler, then in his mid-thirties, had made his mark as an artist and additionally was a skilled sailor in the Boston area. These were precisely the talents the United States Navy needed for a combat artist, reasoned Commander E. John Long, a mutual friend who had taken charge of the Navy's pictorial reporting of the conflict. And so Lt. (jg) Shepler was assigned to duty with the Pacific Fleet as one of our first fighting artists. Given the slim advantage of standing deck watches four-hours-on and twelve-off, instead of the usual four-and-eight, Shep painted intensely as the war raged around him. He saw the carrier *Hornet* go down near Guadalcanal, served there with the embattled Marines, endured the terror of Kamikaze raids, saw duty in the Atlantic and Mediterranean. "I felt I was doing almost no painting," he reminisces of those grim days. Yet three and a half years and a Bronze Star later he had compiled a dramatic history of the war through more than 300 combat scenes. Today they illustrate many definitive accounts of World War II.

Even after VJ-Day, the Navy scheduled one more campaign for its combat artists: to paint a series of murals at my alma mater, the U.S. Naval Academy in Annapolis. His monumental, 30-foot-long "Battle of Santa Cruz" adorned the main entrance to Bancroft Hall.

In the ensuing years I have watched his works spread across the country and to foreign lands, seen them take an honored place in galleries and publications and private collections. I have also grown familiar with his background—the pleasant boyhood in Massachusetts and Maine, studies at Williams College and Boston's School of the Museum of Fine Arts, training under the eminent portraitists Leslie P. Thompson and Harry Sutton, Jr., showings in numerous American museums and in many others abroad, including the National Gallery in London and the Musée de la Marine in Paris. Best of all, over these years, I have acquired a very noble friend.

Just as Shep fought the war that he painted, so he shares a deep personal involvement with other themes that dominate his work. In him we have no detached observer of the passing scene: what he paints, he has also lived. Certainly this intimate involvement translates itself into a vital element of his art.

In the 1930's and '40's he became a pioneer watercolorist of the high ski country. Another artist could easily have glorified the schussers from the comfortable vantage of the lodge. Instead Shep struggled up mountains on skis long before lifts made it easy, and plunged down slopes that were then almost untried. The impact of his winter mountain scenes as they appeared in galleries and in sports publications helped propel skiing to its present awesome popularity. Not surprisingly, the first poster touting the opening of the new Sun Valley ski resort in 1937 was painted by Dwight Shepler.

Somehow, this romance with the highlands has left room for another, perhaps even deeper affection, Shep's life-long love for the sea. And here too he has been the ardent participant. Crewing on a 57-foot staysail schooner in 1936–7, he logged 8,000 miles on a voyage south around the equatorial Galapagos Islands. The 3,600-mile run back to California demanded beating against wind and currents 41 days without anchoring—ample time for testing the durability of one's fondness for the sea.

Often since then he has set up his studio beneath outspread sails. Managing somehow to sketch or paint between attentions to the tiller, he has poked into every cove along the rocky sea edge of New England and Canada's Maritime Provinces. Happily for me, this brought him to Nova Scotia's Bras d'Or Lakes, where we cemented our friendship at my family's summer home in Baddeck. Happily, too, Shep's determined wanderings have yielded a wonderful series of oils and watercolors richly infused with the region's distinctive character. I know this volatile, temperamental country, always changing expression between playful sunshine and frowning fogs, uncertain calms and willful winds. Shep exquisitely captures the moods and the subtleties, be his subject a sea-lashed rock, a bold headland, or the softest lichen on a hoary, wind-tilted old sugar maple.

His involvement in the world he paints has led Dwight Shepler to play a shaping role in an institution dear to the heart of National Geographic—Boston's renowned Museum of Science. For nearly three decades the Society has joined forces with Dr. Bradford Washburn, the Museum's famed director, to support and record his historic mapping explorations of the Mt. McKinley and Mt. Kennedy regions, and now the Grand Canyon. During this time, as the museum has grown to take its place as a major academic institution, Shep has served on its governing body, four years as secretary.

Another institution, the Guild of Boston Artists, also claims a share of Shep's talents and energies. From 1969 to 1973 he has served as president of the Guild, which dates its birth to 1914 during the heyday of the famed "Boston School" of Tarbell, Benson Paxton, De Camp, and the Hales. One can easily sense the satisfaction Shep derives from this organization that furthers the work of some 60 promising regional artists.

"An artist," said Santayana, "is a dreamer consenting to dream in the actual world." As one studies this sensitive selection of Dwight Shepler's works and follows his vastly engaging and underplayed narrative, a conclusion is inescapable: Here is an artist who is both dreamer and doer, and who does them both superbly.

Melville Bell Grosvenor
Editor-in-Chief
Chairman of the Board
National Geographic Society

AN ARTIST'S HORIZONS

D.S.

Percheron. Drawing, 1963, 8″ x 10″.

Finding the Azimuth

When Barre Publishers proposed the idea of publishing a book on my work, with the text as something of a personal record, the result was some searching retrospective reflection as to what impulses and influences formed the varied content assembled in this volume.

Certainly the times, which included the launching of a career during the Great Depression and the Second World War, were an inevitable factor. Contrastingly, the happy and basic experiences of childhood are at the root of many deeply felt themes which matured into paintings. Also, I have long had to admit to myself that what I have accomplished is partly a matter of serendipidity, the hand that other people have taken with my brush. In this tale those Three Princes of Serendip were in the guise of various imaginative and adventurous friends and professional associates, as well as some people I didn't even know. With them I encountered the unexpected on many occasions which have, in various ways, shaped my course.

That painting and drawing were to be my objective was never in question. In that assurance I was fortunate, though carrying it out certainly was tested in the crucible of the Depression. Even in boyhood I was acutely aware of such trends in art as those of the Armory Show of 1913; and, believing that there is more than one way to paint, I have made excursions into various forms. Particularly during my more than three years of combat work for the Navy during World War II, I made tortured and brain-breaking attempts at semi-abstract or allegorical interpretations of what we experienced at sea or on the beach-heads; but they largely proved footling in my own estimation. The fascination and excitement of interpreting the object, the world about and interesting people of our time, has always been the magnet for me. Commencing a watercolor field study is as breathtaking as being in the starting gate of a slalom race in skiing.

Many of these pictures are deeply rooted in Maine and New England. For Maine especially I have always had a perpetual nostalgia, even when right there. In 1908 my father, the Rev. Joseph M. Shepler, D.D., bought a farm for summer use in Windsor, in the agricultural valley of the upper Sheepscot River. He had grown up on a big farm in Ohio, and had to have land under him. The basic experiences of those days, without the trappings of technological advance, are something I would hate to have missed.

The house was a characteristic story-and-a-half early nineteenth century Maine dwelling, standing on a hill under a great elm and overlooking the broad valley through which ran not only the river but the two-foot narrow gauge of the Wiscasset, Waterville and Farmington Railroad. Rounding the bends with high shrill whistle, the small engines pulled an assortment of cars carrying produce and people, much of which was transferred at the Wiscasset terminal to the Maine Central, or to waiting river steamers and coastal schooners.

It was a world of vehicles drawn by horses and oxen, of oil lamps, privies, and no phone. Sparkling cold water came up by hand on the well-curb windlass from a dizzying depth of stoned-up sides of a masterful job of well-building. Way down there, on pieces of clothesline, hung covered lard pails containing milk, butter and other items of refrigeration, and a reflection of one's head. With the planting aid of a neighboring farmer, a seven-acre field was kept in a rotating crop of oats, potatoes and such; while the fields were hayed with horse-drawn mowers, rakes and four-wheeled balustraded racks. My brother Rex and I learned the sweat-encrusted jobs of pitching hay or dusting long rows of spuds, to be rewarded by a swim at the mill dam of Sproul's sawmill. Vegetables from the kitchen garden and the plentiful wild strawberries, blackberries, raspberries and blueberries were canned in jars and packed in barrels for our winter consumption in Boston. A good mess of white perch could be caught in short order from nearby Long Pond.

Occasional gala expeditions were made by carriage and team to such coastal places as Pemaquid; or by narrow gauge and river steamer to Boothbay Harbor, in exchanges of visits with friends. Trips from the steamer landing at Southport, with a lobsterman serving as launch, evoked an early interest in ledge and rockweed in fog and tide, which is still apparent in my recent *On a Maine Reef*, elsewhere in this book.

Another thrill was to drive for postman Les Heisler on his R.F.D. route, the horse actually needing no instructions whatever. We were the only "summerfolk" for miles around, and though we did not face the long winters of our genial neighbors, we did gain an appreciation of their life, and Maine got into my blood.

My mother, Winifred Johnson, was a trained and skilled artist, and it was principally in Maine that she was able to steal time from the duties of a minister's wife to do some painting. Family afflictions sometimes run through generations; ours toward art and architecture have come down through my mother's mother, Ann Dance, from George Dance, one of whose sons, George Dance, Jr., was the first president of the Royal Academy in London. The predilection continues in our artist daughter Joanie and architect son David.

Following a line more or less planned with my parents after Newton High School, I attended the Boston Museum School for a year, graduated from Williams College in 1928, and returned to the Museum School. My principal teachers, Leslie P. Thompson and Philip L. Hale, were excellent teachers and men of colorful intellect, though I chafed a bit at the school's long, formalized program. It was a stirring retrospect in the fall of 1971 to view their reincarnation in the exhibition "The Boston Painters" at the Museum of Fine Arts, and in fact to have had a small hand in its assembling. Along with Thompson and Hale were contemporaries, most of whom I had known and admired: Benson, Bunker, De Camp, Hopkinson, Lillian Wescott Hale, Paxton, Tarbell, Vinton and Woodbury. The April 1972 edition of *American Heritage* commemorates this show in its lead article, "Boston Painters, Boston Ladies," along with many fine color plates.

By 1929 it justly appeared that there had been enough burden of tuitions, even though I worked nights for the Old South Engraving Company-Boston Transcript combination. There followed a free-lance venture into finding some kind of a job to do while sporadically studying oil portrait with Harry Sutton, Jr. He generously came over from Newbury Street to my Chestnut Street studio to give me "crits," and to dissect some of my early attempts at watercolor.

A pot-boiler gaggle of portrait heads for a political advertisement led Russel Gerould, then editor of the Boston Sunday *Herald*, to ask me if I had ever done any writing. I could only reply that as an English major at college I had not received any rave reviews from my professors. Regardless of this, and in the aforementioned spirit of serendipity, he tried me out on a project which continued from 1933 till I entered the Navy early in 1942. This was a series appearing on the editorial pages of the Sunday *Herald*, consisting of a portrait head drawn from life, accompanied by an article, and concerning itself with constructive men and women in the news. Subjects ranged all the way from Serge Koussevitzky to Eddie Shore, bad man of the Boston Bruins. The series was unbeholden to any influence, and its doing was a liberal education.

The accompanying drawing of Frank W. Benson is from that series. The sketch was done in 1935 in his studio on the Riverway, where he had been working on a sparkling big oil of waterfowl. The hand of that great American artist is in this drawing, for when I asked him for a "crit," he said, "Dwight, do you mind? I think that near eye socket should go back a bit— like this." With a fine point of my charcoal he made about a half a dozen light strokes across the area, which can be seen in this excellent reproduction.

During those years of the Depression, paintings were not the most sought-after commodity. The *Sportsman*, edited in Boston by Richard Ely Daniel-

Frank W. Benson. Drawing, 1935, 14″ x 19″.

The HESPER and the LUTHER LITTLE. Watercolor, 1934, 14″ x 21″.

son, and with fine reproduction, offered another out-let. Both Aiden Lassell Ripley, who had a studio across the hall on Chestnut Street, and I were so fortunate as to be virtually staff artists, with many interesting assignments which included mine to cover the Winter Olympics of 1936 at Garmisch in reports and sketches.

The Berkshires of Williamstown elicited some attempts at winter landscapes during college years, but I was a valley-bound hockey player. Skiing was in its infancy, but the coaches, including those of sub-sequent amateur hockey through the World's Cham-pionships in Europe of 1931, wouldn't let us ski. We were getting banged up enough as it was. It was in the winter of 1932 that some friends who had skied at college waxed up a spare pair of skis for me and led me groaning and back-slipping up a mountain in southern Vermont—not as big as it felt. The snow squalls cleared at the summit, revealing a stunning composition. Though the bird's-nesting descent was really easy, it seemed hair-raising to me. However, my heart was high, for I had found a pioneering new theme in snow mountains and skiing.

Early opportunities in cruising under sail ex-panded my appreciation of both the Maine Coast and other New England waters. When we were hardly in our twenties Ken Kepner and Nat Barrows took me on coastwise cruises to Maine and south of the Cape in their small sloops without auxiliary engines, some-times sailing all night. Since then that interest has expanded to distant seas.

It was in 1935, after the incineration of most of the mountain painting production of a couple of winters and of many other watercolors, that I had a few good enough for a one-man show. The subjects were partly from the Laurentians, where, at St. Sau-veur des Monts, I was provided with a studio at the ski lodge of friends, Duke Dimitri and Katia von Leuchtenberg. (see title page) In the thirties the roads were not plowed, but rolled, and all traffic was by sleigh or ski. Other motifs were the Maine Coast's Wiscasset to Port Clyde area. The accompanying plate of The HESPER and the LUTHER LITTLE is one of that group. The now rotting hulks of HESPER and LITTLE have become Wiscasset's "Motif Number One." As I saw them then they were intact, and had just been grounded out on a spring tide in a mud berth alongside the pier trestle of my beloved and just then defunct narrow gauge.

The focus of retrospect centers on the year 1935. It was then that the channels of my effort appear to have merged into a presentable offering. I felt that I was strong in drawing, particularly in portrait, where by circumstance I had derived so much experience; but in the medium of oil my portraits were still to be under the bushel for several more years.

Therefore, it is in 1935, when I was six years out of college and art school, that this book begins.

Weston, Massachusetts

Docks at Menemsha Basin. Watercolor, 1961, 20½″ x 29″.

PART I

Down East and Other Courses

My introduction to extended blue-water cruising came in 1936–37 aboard Charles J. Hubbard's 57-foot staysail schooner ZAVORAH, circling the southern part of the North American continent, with a diversion along the coasts of Colombia and Ecuador and to the Galapagos Islands.

Charlie had used ZAVORAH as a base ship while he carried out the second summer of Dr. Alexander Forbes' aerial mapping of the Labrador coast for the American Geographical Society in 1932. During World War II these two men planned and established the air bases of the northern air route to the European Theatre. Hubbard was a twice All-American tackle and captain at Harvard, a fine scholar and a man of astounding versatility. My mother said he was born four hundred years too late, for he was at heart an explorer. It was as head of the Arctic Weather Project for the United States Weather Bureau that in 1951 he was killed in the line of duty in the crash of a Royal Canadian Air Force re-supply plane at the northernmost weather station of Alert, on the edge of the polar sea.

At Woods Hole we re-rigged ZAVORAH to a staysail schooner with fisherman topsail. On the foremast we installed a yard to which was bent a big squaresail, with triangular raffee above. With wind on the port quarter this rig, plus gaff main and staysails, was to boost us along over the great trade-wind seas from Kingston, Jamaica, to the Panama Canal in three days and seven hours, at hull speed. The painting *Sextant Sight* shows the bottom of the square-sail only slightly braced around, almost dead before the wind in Pacific swells.

The final leg of just over 3,600 sea miles from the Galapagos to California was sailed in forty-one days without dropping the hook, there being no adequate place to do so. After leaving the doldrum areas near the lone atoll of Clipperton Island, where we stood on and off the reefs to fish, we were hard on the wind in the northeast trades for three weeks on the starboard tack, and another week tacking in to the coast at San Pedro, port of Los Angeles. Young Robin Graham, in the final passage of his round-the-world voyage in his sloop DOVE, sailed this same course in thirty-eight days, three days faster. One would think such a long board would be tedious, but with ZA-VORAH's sail plan trimmed so that she virtually sailed herself, I found that the time passed profitably in reading, sketching and reflection. We all had visions of what we would eat when we got ashore, but when it came to pass I found myself selecting a full order of ham and eggs.

Reggie cleans a fish

FULL CIRCLE 'ROUND

The narrative returns to the point of ZA-VORAH's departure, to Woods Hole, the Elizabeth Islands and Vineyard Sound. The chain of Nonamesset, Naushon, Pasque, Nashawena and Cuttyhunk, with moorland, forest, dune, with strong tidal currents through the holes separating them, have a form and atmosphere of haunting splendor.

Due to the generosity of Alex and Dave Forbes I have painted a great deal on and about Naushon; in fact our family used a house there for a time one autumn. Dr. Alex, whom I have already mentioned as an aerial cartographer, was a noted physiologist at Harvard Medical School as well. Some years we helped him sail his big ketch STORMSVALA to or from his easterly habitat, a camp house at Burnt Coat Harbor in Maine. Though he was a generation older than I, it never seemed so—so young was his spirit.

The families who inhabit Naushon allocate a relatively small part of the island to houses, stock or tillage, the remainder being in its natural state of growth and wildlife. Motor vehicles of strictly a work sort can be counted on one hand. All other locomotion is on foot or horseback, or by carriage. This slow pace unfolds scenes of wonder.

On an autumn morning, sprayed by showers and shafts of sunlight, three of us were riding with Dave in a carriage behind Tess, a gentle black mare. The narrow road became obstructed by a recent hurricane windfall, so a roadless detour found Tess approaching a steep meadow knoll, where three of us alighted to reduce her load. As Dave, arrayed in an old orange foul-weather jacket and a black fisherman's rain hat, drove on up to the height of land, the perspective was compelling. On a latter day my wife Hennie and I harnessed up Tess, re-enacting the scene as I made watercolor and pencil sketches from which emerged the large watercolor entitled *Tess*.

It is interesting that behind Tess, or on horseback, one sees much more of wildlife than when trudging along with a rucksack of painting gear. The softest human tread spreads far more alarm than the beat of the hoof. Wild turkeys, deer and smaller animals abound. The "Horseman in Witches' Glen," as depicted in the accompanying painting, headed possibly for Billiard Table Road and Tarpaulin Cove, will observe more fauna than the artist scrambling up a rock behind him. From his mount he also surveys, beyond the moors, the sweep of Vineyard Sound, Menemsha Basin, and the varicolored cliffs of Gay Head on Martha's Vineyard. An indigenous scene of the Vineyard is that of *Docks at Menemsha*.

On the horizon beyond Cuttyhunk, in the waters off Brenton's Reef, there has been re-enacted for over a century the successful defense of the America's Cup. The watercolor *INTREPID vs. DAME PATTIE, with AMERICA* portrays the drama of match racing on a windward leg in the series of 1967. The defender, keeping her opponent covered, crosses her opponent by a length, with right of way on the starboard tack, the razor edge of design and sailing skill which overcame the gallant "Aussies." Clear of the wind is Rudolph Schaefer's replica of AMERICA, the schooner which started the whole thing. It is a matter of fierce local pride for one whose hailing port is East Boothbay, that she was built there by Goudy and Stevens.

Quality in a painting is not measured by verisi-

Tess. Watercolor, 1960, 20½″ x 29″.

militude alone, but what makes one boat different from another one designed under the 12-meter rule can be the width of a line in the sheer of INTREPID's deck. Olin Stevens' snubby bow, however, is distinctive. The painting was commissioned by Samuel Wakeman for his son, Samuel W. Wakeman, a member of INTREPID's crew. Both Wakemans have long been involved with the America's Cup, having crewed for Chandler Hovey's EASTERNER in earlier Cup trials. Shipbuilder Sam, Sr., was in charge of the construction of the last of the great J Boats, Harold Vanderbilt's RANGER, at the Bath Iron Works in Maine in 1937. Designed by W. Starling Burgess with the assistance of young Olin Stevens, she is said to be the fastest single-hulled yacht which ever sailed, or probably ever will.

W. Starling Burgess. Drawing, 1935, 16″ x 12″.

Horseman in Witches' Glen. Watercolor, 1960, 20½″ x 29″.

INTREPID vs. DAME PATTIE, with AMERICA. Watercolor, 1968, 20¾″ x 29¼″.

DOWN EAST IS DOWN WIND

The coast of Maine, as everybody knows, has everything: searock and pine tree, surf and snug harbors, lighthouse and steeple, lofty mountain, saltwater farms, islands and fog. Mr. Shepler, who can sail as well as he can ski or travel, is aware of this. One layman would cite his particular gift for combining action and tranquility: reflection in the tide rip, the fingers of fog at the throat of a village, tailwind on a sail, seamarks and sea breeze. Such little passages of poetry give depth to watercolors, particularly when all is low in tone. Fog is low in tone, but how beautiful it can be. Sunshine will speak for itself.

DAVID MCCORD

In the early days of New England almost all travel and commerce to and from Maine and the Maritime Provinces of Canada was by sea in sailing ships. The trend of the shoreline coupled with the tip of the ship's magnetic compass to nineteen degrees and more of westerly variation combine to give the navigator base courses of approximately east or west. The prevailing southwesterly wind, on which I comment twice later, sent the square riggers and the schooners flying to the eastward on a broad reach, their best angle of sailing, and in a sailor's terms, down wind.

During the remaining pages of Part One, we embark on a cruise Down East with a skeleton crew of brush and typewriter.

To me Down East begins at Cape Porpoise and becomes more vividly so beyond. The heavily indented shore line of Maine measures a total of about 2,500 miles, while literally hundreds of islands dot its bays or lie offshore. After almost fifty years of cruising there and many paintings later, I still have much more to see.

David McCord, in the generous commentary quoted above, speaks of "seamarks and sea breezes." One of the great seamarks seen sailing eastward is the towering, barren island of Seguin, clothed in tawny low growth where not sheer rock, and a stunning composition from many angles. In the watercolor entitled *Seguin* the coaster schooner SILVER HEELS is working her way to the westward in Sheepscot Bay, inside the island and toward the tide rips off the mouth of the mighty Kennebec. This painting was effected by dousing sail on two or three occasions when sun and wind were right, and drifting about while making drawings and color notes.

Bending on new mainsail, Gertrude L. Thebaud
D.S. Sept. 1938

On Passing Seguin. Watercolor, 1968, 21″ x 29″.

Flood Tide, Boulder Island. Watercolor, 1970, 14½″ x 21″.

On such a day SILVER HEELS has witnessed a panoply of sights now astern in her wake, but still ahead on our course: the sweep of bays and wide river entrances, islands such as Monhegan and Damariscove to seaward, or ledges with such expressive names as The Hypocrites. Of these immediate rivers—Kennebec, Sheepscot and Damariscotta—the latter is more of a fjord than a river, its eight to ten feet of tide containing only a small amount of fresh water from Damariscotta Lake. The flood tide, crowding through the narrows at Fort Island, reaches six knots, causing the huge red nun buoy to porpoise, thrash and sometimes sound like a whale for embarrassing lengths of time.

The glaciers of the ice age scoured out these channels, traced by oceanographic transducers to the edge of the continental shelf.

Halfway up the river the glacier fashioned a motif for artists and photographers, situated at the foot of the steep meadow of the saltwater farm where our family has summered for twenty-six years. The continuation of a small point becomes just barely an island at high tide, with a stone pier and float at its end. A study of its anatomy reveals that it is a small ridge of huge boulders piled on top of each other, and crowned with thin topsoil through which gnarled little oaks, pine and spruce of oriental mien reach roots down into the crevices. Just under high water level near the footbridge grows the subtle sea lavender, while at low tide the wrack clings to the big stones and drifts on its small floats.

Too small for a name on the chart, this land is ycleped Boulder Island by this artist in search for a title for paintings of it in several moods and tides. The paper reproduced, *Flood Tide, Boulder Island,* reflects the joy of a Maine summer day.

The sailor entering the Damariscotta might instead be headed into Johns Bay through Thread of Life Passage. This narrow, deep slot is formed by a line of ledges and ledge islands running parallel to the peninsula of Rutherford Island, and on out to seaward, culminating in the stark Thrumcap Island. These ledges with varied rock formations offer many interesting motifs. At certain stages of tide a lobsterman with local knowledge can weave between some of them, a practice which can prove non-habit-forming for a keel vessel. They are low ghosts in the fog when one is making a landfall on Thrumcap; stubby vegetation clings to some of them, while Crow Island on the inshore end is capped with spruce.

In a fresh sou'wester the wind draws right through this slot, and it can be a sportive ride, dodging lobster pot buoys and lobstermen while making a hopefully controlled jibe at the end to spew out between the nun and can buoys into Johns Bay. Beyond, near the middle of the bay, lies Johns Island. In a bygone year a sailor emerging from Thread of Life might have witnessed H.M.S. Gun Brig BOXER behind Johns Island, weighing anchor for her fateful engagement with ENTERPRISE III.

Lobstermen, Thread of Life. Watercolor, 1958, 19¾″ x 38″.

It may seem anachronistic suddenly to brace the yards aback against the winds of time for more than a century and a half, but the memory of that action is kept green by coast inhabitants, fishermen and sailors who sometimes can almost hear those carronades, booming through the smoky sou'wester.

The title of the accompanying large oil can easily be read in the fine reproduction, in the legend lettered on the navy blue panel of Leon Brathwaite's specially designed frame. The painting was commissioned along with one of the great nuclear-powered aircraft carrier U.S.S. ENTERPRISE in 1961. In February 1972 I went aboard the carrier in San Francisco to find this work unscathed and firmly secured to the bulkhead of the officers' mess.

This title also might be *The First Monhegan Island Ocean Race, 1813.* for the summer weather pattern proved quite similar to those considered on the final leg to Casco Bay, on rounding the Monhegan whistler about dawn after the long eastward leg from Cape Porpoise.

Captain William Burrows' victory in 1813 over gallant Captain Samuel Blyth was largely one of anticipation, local knowledge and seamanship. Our sloop's hailing port is nearby East Boothbay, so this action has always been of great interest, as it was to Mr. Franke. The research was engrossing and more time-consuming than the painting, culminating in a long paper on the subject, with course plots on chart No. 314. Because of unseamanly discrepancies in various accounts, I had gone back to original sources.

This recourse to sources led to reefs under the keel of scholarship. When I wrote to my friend Rear Admiral E.M. Eller, USN, Chief of Naval Records and History, for a transcript of the log of ENTERPRISE for September 5, 1813, he ruefully replied that all logs of U.S. naval vessels are missing from the archives for the period 22 June to 16 September, 1813. Secondly, old prints or paintings of the action demonstrated that delineations of the gun brig BOXER were purely conjectural; for she had never swung for her portrait by Antoine Roux, being virtually destroyed in this action off the Maine Coast less than a year after her commissioning.

Our ship of research seemed almost lost, when a rising tide of good fortune lifted her off the first obstacle. At the Peabody Museum of Salem Mr. Marion V. Brewington, curator of maritime research, led me to Volume XXXII, *Naval Chronicles*, Royal Navy, 1814. This publication contained direct quotes from the log of the senior surviving officer, Lieutenant Edward R. McCall, USN, in an interview following the action recorded by the Portland, Maine, *Argus*. The National Maritime Museum of Greenwich, England, kedged us off the second shoal by miraculously producing white prints of the naval architect's original plans of H.M.S. BOXER.

In brief, the story is that ENTERPRISE, in quest of BOXER, sailed from Casco Bay near Portland and found herself offshore near Monhegan Island at daylight. From that position she sighted the masts of what proved to be BOXER, anchored behind Johns Island in Johns Bay, which makes in to the westward of Pemaquid Point. There was a light norther, N by W.

This is where that matter of weather conditions comes into play. The wind referred to could be due to one of two familiar reasons, either of which can lead to the breeze going into the prevailing WSW. In

Presented to U.S.S. ENTERPRISE VIII on her commissioning by Bertha R. Franke, wife of William B. Franke, Secretary of the Navy 1959-61

The victorious engagement of U.S. gun brig ENTERPRISE with H.B.M.'s brig BOXER off Pemaquid Point, Maine, September 5, 1813

ENTERPRISE and BOXER. Oil, 1961, 30″ x 40″.

periods of several days of warm weather, the morning norther often comes down the rivers and bays, off the land. This peters out into calms as the heat of the land begins to draw in the sou'wester. Or as noted in *Off Frenchman Bay*, page 50, the northwester of an ebbing high pressure system can give way to the inevitable WSW. (On October 2, 1972, a few days before this was written, my wife and I had moored at Monhegan for the night, and while sailing toward the mainland late the next morning, experienced the exact phenomena of the first instance.)

Having sighted the unidentified brig, ENTER-PRISE worked her way inshore. Veteran crew were skeptical of new skipper Burrows' courage, for he had a long nine ranged out of his cabin windows in the stern. As his enemy approached, Blyth hoisted ensigns in pursuit of Burrows, who bore off seaward in the light air; the winds became fitful, the ships nearly motionless. As afternoon progressed the sou'wester strengthened, and both brigs tacked to windward in the very flat tacks to which the square rig was limited. Holding the weather gauge, and "covering" her opponent, ENTERPRISE eased sheets on the starboard tack and bore off with superior speed to engage broadsides at pistol shot range. Carrying her way she ranged ahead to rake BOXER fore and aft with the long nine out the stern ports. Bearing off, then rounding up, ENTERPRISE unmasked the seven unused carronades of her starboard broadside, reducing BOXER to a hulk.

The gallant Blyth was killed in the rigging as the action opened, and Burrows was mortally wounded soon after. Both captains lie buried side by side in a Portland cemetery. Several United States naval ships have been named after both BOXER and Burrows.

Pleasant Point Gut. Watercolor, 1972, 8½″ x 14¾″.

The Osprey Nest. Watercolor, 1963, 23½″ x 36¼″.

Beyond Pemaquid Point, Muscongus Bay makes in with its many islands and coves. Our small cruising sloop GRAMPUS serves as a sort of floating studio along the coast, while aboard her my wife and I have criss-crossed Muscongus in every direction: subject matter is all about. I would hate to lose my place in the fog there, and once thought I had; for the waters contain such awesomely-named sunken foreign bodies as the Devil's Limb, the Devil's Elbow and the Devil's Back. The comber roused by the Devil's Back can be a frightening but valuable navigational fix.

Friendship, renowned for its historic lobster sloops and the Friendship Sloop revival races held there every year, is at the head of the bay, while at the broad entrance of the St. George River is a much-favored anchorage, Pleasant Point Gut. One year while cruising I went ashore to find a telephone, and as there is no store nor public booth, I followed wires to a house just by the spot where later in 1971 I painted the accompanying watercolor. The very dear old lady whose phone I used responded to my thanks by saying, "I think it is part of our business here at Pleasant Point to be friendly one to another."

Overlooking the next anchorage up the St. George Maple Juice Cove is Olson's House, in the country of Andrew Wyeth, an associate since the days when his first shows at Doll and Richards in Boston predicted his marvelous career. Two or three years ago our binoculars revealed, from a bit offshore, those rags still stuffed in the third story gable window, as limned in his painting *Weather Side*.

The osprey, or fish hawk, with his wingspread of four-and-a-half to six feet, is a sight comparable to the bald eagle. His soaring flight is interrupted by a plunging dive to catch a fish in his talons, after which he flies back to the nest looking like a torpedo bomber, and talking about it. The gyrations of one transporting a big struggling eel are even more spectacular, his incongruous high cry audible from even a long way to windward.

Though I am not a qualified "bird knocker," endless hours spent observing these magnificent creatures have resulted in a couple of paintings on the subject. The nest in the plate is from a detailed drawing of one on Carlisle Island, which could be studied closely from a good height of eye. These avian basket-weavers use all kinds of materials—branches, keg staves, a section of hose or whatever takes their fancy—to fashion these huge observation posts which last for season after season. The watercolor *The Osprey Nest* was motivated on the Damariscotta, but is a "dream-up" which could be set in many places in Maine.

In twenty-six years of observation on the Damariscotta I have found that this elsewhere seriously threatened species has now regained a maximum yet to be estimated. Never before the last two summers have we seen six or seven soaring together as they now do, suddenly aroused by the slatting sail of a boat coming about near the bold shore.

SEAMARK ROCKS AND MOUNTAIN TOPS

Pulpit Harbor, on North Haven Island, is a Maine classic. In a prospect more familiar than the accompanying watercolor, the main harbor faces out to Penobscot Bay and the Camden Hills through its narrow entrance, with Pulpit Rock, osprey nest atop, dividing the approach.

Some years ago an idiot in an out-of-state power cruiser shot an osprey on the Pulpit nest, which thereupon remained uninhabited for several seasons. On a subsequent summer night a couple of boys rowed out and set fire to the huge nest, which made a most satisfactory beacon. The pair of pyromaniacs were detected on coming ashore, and roundly punished. It proved they had done man and bird a favor, for after this incineration of all traces of tragedy, ospreys returned, built a new residence, and now greet the sailor with their high cries.

The painting somewhat reorganizes what you see when looking across a branch of the main harbor sometimes known as "Cabot's Creek." Paul Cabot, who owns the watercolor, remarks, "They tell me that I have been looking at this view for seventy-two years."

Cabot's Creek, Pulpit Harbor. Watercolor, 1971, 21″ x 29¼″.

The 44-foot yawl CIRRUS, which plays a leading part in this Down East cruise over paper waves, is portrayed preparing to leave her hailing port on Egge-moggin Reach, that lovely strait between Deer Isle and the mainland.

This swift and powerful vessel is one of the great designs of the late Nat Herreshoff, originally built as a Fisher's Island sloop to very high specifications. Her smooth cadmium red hull with flashing sheer strake of varnished teak was formed in 1930. Alan Bemis has owned her since 1934. In 1970 and 1971 she flew the flag of Commodore of the Cruising Club of America, a flag more likely to be seen on one of the latest products of the designer's board.

In 1954 Alan converted her to yawl rig at Frankie Day's yard at nearby Benjamin River, which involved shortening the boom at the aft end. Frankie Day measured, made a mark and handed over the saw.

"You'd better do it. I might get it cock-eyed," said Bemis.

"I won't cut it off!" protested Frankie.

"Why?"

"Well, with all the changes you been makin' in this vessel I won't make Uncle Nat turn over in his grave again."

The yawl BRENDA is going places under mizzen staysail and all while reaching past a Maine ledge island. At the time of her portrait she belonged to Jim Madden; she was later succeeded by his 57-foot sloop GESTURE, and now GESTURE II. Designed by John Alden, she was 45 feet overall, 8 foot beam and 6 foot draft. Fast, close-winded and able, she was also wet! We who crewed aboard her in ocean races were accused by our Navy-type competitors of drawing "submarine pay." All 45 feet of her were steered by a tiller.

In an informal race BRENDA was footing down wind under all her dimity—spinnaker, spinnaker stay-sail, main, mizzen and mizzen staysail—when skipper Madden announced that we were going to have to jibe. Contemplating the maze of sheets, guys, halyards and back-stays, the captain's wife Pauline exclaimed, "Oh, the strings! the strings! so many strings!"

BRENDA appears later in this narrative in comments about Lunenburg Harbor.

Departure of CIRRUS. Watercolor, 1963, 10″ x 14¼″.

BRENDA. Watercolor, 1959, 21″ x 29″.

Efforts to record one's own young at various stages of growing up causes almost more fidgeting and alleged hardship than when one is getting paid for the job.

However, at this stage in the life of daughter Joanie, who is now a professional artist, it was a different matter, for she was keenly interested. Her only drawback to sitting there was that she couldn't watch at the same time. The painting is a 40 x 30 inch panel, on a textured polymertempera ground, and underpainting. The medium is basically oil. For those interested in the permanency of techniques, this work shows no evidence of change or deterioration in thirteen years: such trends would have started by now.

This summer study was painted in the studio in the small dance hall above Burnham's former general store in nearby East Edgecomb, where I had installed a big north window. "Wallflower" benches lined the long dimensions under beautiful oil lamps in brackets. A big, square grand piano still stood in the corner. One could almost hear its notes over the squeal of the fiddle and the caller's cant.

The shoemaker's child didn't get any shoes, but the artist's child will get the portrait in the end.

Joan. Oil, 1959, 40″ x 30″.

Dale. Drawing, 1969.

The watercolor *On a Maine Reef* is a by-product of my yanking the lower gudgeon out of the transom of the little BRUTAL BEAST, as I grazed the rocks too close at mid-tide. The bronze gudgeon which dropped off the pintle of the removable rudder is such a specialized little fitting that it takes weeks on order.

Early the next morning at dead low water I set forth in the dinghy to look for this object on the reef. It was just after dawn in a dungeon of fog. Having pinpointed the scene of the crime, surprisingly soon I found the greeny-brown bronze gudgeon, playing chameleon in rockweed of the same color.

The reef was a wondrous place in that mood, and I sat still there for a long time as the big tide crept up. This was a world of seals, gulls, and cormorants, and of irascible terns who dove at me, though there could be no territorial imperative of nesting on this reef which is underwater at flood tide. These revelations led me to return there several times to make studies.

On the row of a few hundred yards back to the pier a half dozen seals, with their big curious eyes, followed the dinghy almost all the way.

On a Maine Reef. Watercolor, 1961, 21¼″ x 29½″.

The portrait of Samuel Eliot Morison, the great historian and teacher, hangs in the St. Botolph Club in Boston, in company with that of historian Francis Parkman by Frederick Vinton, and of Robert Frost by Gardner Cox. He relates to this book in several contexts, but this part on the northeast coast and the Caribbean seems most germane.

The reproduction of this portrait appropriately appears near the plate *Off Frenchman Bay,* for it is at Northeast Harbor that Morison spends much of his year writing, when he is not following the track of the explorers under sail, under steam, or with aerial camera. In the book *Spring Tides* he recounts his cruising experiences Down East. His classic *Admiral of the Ocean Sea* (1942) recounts his following of the courses of Columbus, under sail. The latest of his many works, *The European Discovery of North America—The Northern Voyages* (1971) is soon to be followed by *The Southern Voyages.* With the extraordinary vitality of his eighty-six years, he also managed to fit in a book about Champlain.

His fifteen volume opus, *History of United States Naval Operations in World War II* contains, in the final volume color plates of some of my paintings shown in the last part of this book. Several paintings were also adapted as jackets of the Morison volumes, along with works by esteemed cohort Official U.S. Navy Combat Artists: Commander Griffith Bailey Coale, Lieutenant Commander William F. Draper, Lieutenant Mitchell Jamieson, and Commander Albert K. Murray, all USNR.

Rear Admiral Samuel Eliot Morison. Oil, composite dates, 44″ x 34″.

Of Maine's many treasures, Mount Desert Island is probably its greatest. The full impact of its grandeur can only be realized when one approaches from the sea, as did Champlain, who named it. On the sailing passage from Cape Sable, Nova Scotia, one's landfall is on the summit of Cadillac Mountain as it appears on the horizon. From that moment the panoply unfolds as one peak after another join to form the massif rising sheer from the ocean.

This composition of Cadillac, Dorr and Champlain mountains is one choice; while approaches through Western Way or up the fjord of Somes Sound offer a myriad of other motifs. A morning's northwester is still over the land mass, but off Frenchman Bay the prevailing summer sou'wester is beginning to build in, the water a fitful miscellany of calms and puffs. It was in anticipating this weather characteristic that Burrows defeated Blyth as described in ENTERPRISE vs. BOXER, page 36. Off Otter Cliffs and under water in the left foreground is the rock which Champlain struck, not having aboard C. and G. S. Chart No. 306, which now marks it with a bell buoy. Fitting to the scene is Roger Duncan's Friendship Sloop EASTWARD, whose ubiquitous owner is the author-in-chief of the yachtsman's bible, *The Cruising Guide to the New England Coast*, as was his father Bob before him.

Off Frenchman Bay. Watercolor, 1972, 20″ x 29″.

This full-sheet watercolor was developed from four studies made over several years, while on the course from Eastern Way to the Schoodic whistle buoy. Substantially completed in June 1972, it hung in our living room in Boothbay for further critique. It was a breathtaking moment in August when I found myself drifting along aboard CIRRUS under the exact circumstances of the painting. I found that in the mood of the day, the anatomy of the land and sea, I hadn't been lying. That sou'wester picked up, and soon we were crossing Petit Manan Bar.

There is not a strip of sand worth mentioning between Pemaquid and Roque, that incomparably romantic island which is the Ultima Thule of the blue-water sailor. On the seaward side of this generally H-shaped island curves the mile-long sweep of soft white sand of the Great Beach. The Gardner family, who have owned the island for generations, are hospitable in allowing boatsmen to use the north end of the beach, to swim if hardy enough, to roam the wood paths and climb the high eminences.

It is difficult to encompass what one sees and feels at Roque. One of several attempts is this 1972 watercolor of the spruce-covered cliff of an inner headland with part of the sweep of the beach.

There was a time when I took the Maine Coast for granted, as I did magnificent Vermont dairy barns and high pastures, but for a long while now I haven't. Beyond Roque and through Foster Channel one enters broad Machias Bay. Off to starboard is Cross Island, and almost on course to port the spectacular spruce-crowned headland of Stone Island. Only very recently this island and the adjacent Starboard Island and Point of Main were saved from being destroyed by a projected deep water oil port storage and refinery. Despite the immediate needs of man, our generation is not entitled to erase the irreplaceable and unique natural assets and resources of the coast of Maine.

The Great Beach, Roque Island. Watercolor, 1973, 14″ x 20″.

FOG

Piloting in the fog is a specialized craft necessary to cruising Down East. There can be gorgeous days on end, but then there are the ones when the offshore fog bank moves in, or dense fog patches form suddenly.

"Pride cometh before a fall," and as Dick Preston says, "A little *local* knowledge is a dangerous thing." This puts to mind a yarn told to me by old Maine carpenter friend Will Poole. Henry Harrington had been captain of one of the river steamers, and, when they went out, he took on some local piloting jobs. "He was bringin' a power launch up the Damariscotty in a thick o' fog," related Will, "and braggin' what a pilot he was—knowed every rock in the river. Just then he struck. 'Well, there's one right now!' says Henry."

This fog business would be a lot easier if the water, not the waves, would only hold still, for you are on a moving platform of tidal current, sometimes moving fast. You can easily fool yourself in trying to crank this into your dead reckoning. There are many techniques, such as timing the echo of your horn from a bold shore, or steaming in a circle to set up centrifugal wave patterns to induce a sound buoy to talk in a calm. The sound of surf, the sight of its white line, the cry of gulls are other clues in the practice of deliberately sailing at a bold headland or steep-to rock, for a new departure. Breasting the strong tides in and out of the Bay of Fundy, midway between Cross Island and Cutler, is just such a target, Old Man Island. It is really a huge rock, capped by a few spruces rendered scraggly by a populous gull colony; it usually sets up quite a bother of surf, and when seen abeam has an unmistakable cleft down its center.

All this at least tells you where you are for the time being, and is the motivation of the study *Landfall on Old Man.*

Landfall on Old Man. Drawing, 1969, 10″ x 13″.

The lighthouse at East Quoddy Head on Campobello Island guards the easterly approaches to Passamaquoddy Bay, its big red cross on two sides a welcome sight to many a mariner. In the painting, the beamy yawl MEMORY sets forth out of Head Harbor into the fog patches.

This all brings up my favorite true fog story. On return from the 1965 Cruising Club Cruise to Saint John River, New Brunswick, the yawls CIRRUS and GAY GULL III, because of committee duties, were the last boats of a large fleet through the Reversing Falls and out of Saint John Harbor. The next destination was a rendezvous and customs re-entry at Head Harbor. It was foggy in the Bay of Fundy. CIRRUS, departing about a half hour before GAY GULL, picked up the offshore buoys at Point Lepreau and The Wolves, and, well after dark, the lighthouse at East Quoddy. The big diaphone nearly blasted us off the deck from close aboard as we followed the bold starboard shore into the long, narrow harbor. An unaccountable weak light appeared ahead in the dense gloom, at an elevation of about ten feet. It proved to be on the boat of a weir fisherman who had moored her off his new weir, for both its protection and that of the arriving fleet.

Shortly after we had moored, GAY GULL ghosted in and rafted alongside. When queried as to the mysterious light, skipper Bob Love said, "Yes, indeed! I had Hugh (Sharp) up on the bow, and when he yelled that he saw a light I asked him if he could tell what it was. Hugh leaned out over the pulpit, groped all around and shouted back, "It feels like a boat!"

Fog at East Quoddy Head. Watercolor, 1967, 23″ x 38″.

OUTER ISLANDS, OUTER HAVENS

There is a theme within the theme of coastal Maine; that of the outer islands, the offshore course.

Far off the mouth of Penobscot Bay lies Matinicus, a name that has come to connote a distant and genuine world of seafarers. Approached from Monhegan this low island can be seen from only ten miles' distance in good visibility, while on a course out from Vinalhaven it is quite a while before it appears on the horizon in the open ocean. The inhabitants of Matinicus are their own men and women in their own friendly world, with their big powerful lobster boats, well-kept ancient dock buildings, taut little houses around the small harbor. The history of Matinicus is as old as any part of the coast, for Captain John Smith sent fishing schooners to Matinicus during the days of the Jamestown Colony in Virginia.

Once when visiting Matinicus in Ralph Williams' ketch RANGER I started off on a study in bright sunlight, but before I got very far the fog began to roll in and certain elements of the composition became faint or disappeared entirely. Things were still mighty interesting, so it ended up in that mood. The following day I anticipated that the fog was going to burn off, so I started drawing on the basis of what I had in the first study and, *mirabile dictu*, the subject I started in the first instance emerged, eventually to be developed into the accompanying *Cove at Matinicus*.

Out even to seaward of Matinicus, towards Matinicus Rock and the nestings of puffins, is the island of Criehaven, its anchorage somewhat sheltered by a lighted breakwater, and fairly secure in anything other than a northwester.

While I was working on the watercolor *Outermost Harbor*, the wild, remote feeling of the place spurred me on to virtual completion of the paper on the spot. There was something of the atmosphere of Naushon, but more that of the Outer Hebrides. To landward the low profile of Matinicus appears.

At anchor in the cove that night we witnessed fervid excitement in the darkness as, with dashing boats and flashing searchlights, the fishermen strung a net across the harbor entrance to trap a big school of herring. The following morning they obligingly dipped a section for us to get out, with our centerboard up.

There is tiny Duck Harbor at the outer end of Isle au Haut, while on beyond is another bent French name which seems to have been corrupted from Côte Brûlé into Burnt Coat Harbor, on the seaward shore of big Swan's Island. It is classically Maine, a wonderful anchorage to which we have sailed many a time. The watercolor *Burnt Coat Revisited* was done long ago, in 1950, and its owner just brought it to the studio this morning for use in this volume.

This is one of several paintings I have done at Burnt Coat, but the sight of this one fills me with nostalgia; there are so many aspects of it that have significance. The channel in the distance is the lesser entrance, a narrow twisting affair, and beyond is Spain. On entering this one day Alex Forbes got a bit familiar and put STORMSVALA's forefoot on a sharp rock, right in his own front yard; for the camp house I mentioned in the text about Naushon is on Harbor Island, directly behind the larger sail. The resultant gouge, just above the lead, later proved ideal

58

Outermost Harbor, Criehaven. Watercolor, 1963, 14½″ x 21″.

for catching a long string of lobster pots which served as a good sea anchor, and occasioned diving work on the part of this crew.

It is hard to improve on Burnt Coat as a composition, except for transplanting a tree or two and moving GOLDEN HIND's anchorage a bit. Just around the small island is where Ted Buswell then lived, a lobsterman of strong and genial character. They say a lobsterman never gets lost in the fog. He obligingly took us to Stonington one time for land transportation, the fog mull thickening in Deer Island Thorofare. Ted then remarked he hadn't been to Stonington for five years, hardly ever went there; furthermore he had no chart. "Pay a dollah for one of them, and the first thing you know you're off'n it." After getting off into a dead-end cove we finally made it in. Ted later reported that getting home was a cinch.

The schooner at anchor was George and Peggy Clowes' GOLDEN HIND, in which the year before we made a passage from Falmouth, Cape Cod, to Halifax, then along the coast to Cape Breton Island and the Bras d'Or.

The full-sheet watercolor at Grand Manan with all the comings and goings was derived from sketches while doing just that on two or three occasions. The tall sloop has just come out of the breakwaters of North Head Harbor, from behind Swallowtail Light, while the handsome work boat is bound there. The fog bank hangs off shore. The fishermen of Grand Manan have fine vessels and are admirable people. One year aboard CIRRUS, when wind and tide were foul in Grand Manan Channel, we came around to North Head Harbor via the awesome archipelago of islands and reefs on the seaward side of the big island. We relied upon fishermen for local knowledge in these huge tides and currents, stopping at both Seal Harbor and at Grand Harbor, where we rafted inside the breakwater, outboard of two trawlers. The skipper of the well-found boat we were tied to invited us aboard. The investment in fish-finding sonar equipment and other electronics on his bridge must have taken a lot of fish to pay for; his taut galley-cabin with big stove would have been the envy of any housewife ashore. He offered us a drink, but declined one himself, as he said he was expecting his crew soon and was going out that night. This he did, slipping his lines and securing ours to the inner boat while waking only one of our crew—not this one.

Burnt Coat Revisited. Watercolor, 1950, 14½″ x 21¼″.

Cove at Matinicus. Watercolor, 1965, 15″ x 21½″.

Swallowtail Light, Grand Manan. Watercolor, 1963, 20″ x 28½″.

OF INLAND SEAS, AND RIVERS

"Little Letite, Little L'Étang,
Digdeguash and Grand Manang!"

This exultation of Buzz Amory, an early sailor to Passamaquoddy Bay, expresses his joy and that of his followers on entering those waters. Passamaquoddy is one of three remarkable and almost land-locked cruising areas of Eastern Maine and the Atlantic Maritime Provinces of Canada; the others are Saint John River, New Brunswick, and the Bras d'Or Lakes of Cape Breton Island.

Passamaquoddy is virtually shut off from the sea by islands, between which are such entrances as Letite and Little Letite Passages, Lubec Narrows. In fair weather there are wonderful skies, even though it might be foggy out to sea. There are many coves and inlets with inviting names which roll off the tongue rhythmically, if you can pronounce them: Bocabec, Digdeguash, Midjik Bluff and Magaguadavic River (pronounced Macadavie). At the mouth of this inlet we once saw a spectacular altercation in flight between an osprey and a bald eagle. Islands such as McMaster's and Pendleton present handsome red and ochre cliffs for the brush of the painter. The fisherman-farmer owners of a family compound at Bocabec Cove once invited us to help ourselves to their vegetable crops.

Cobscook Bay, an offshoot of Passamaquoddy, comprises almost half of this labyrinthine inland water, its inner reaches being approached through the Cobscook Falls. At mid-flood tide it is quite a slalom on a 45-foot yawl, negotiating the S-turn past Roaring Bull and Guv'ment Rock, but the compressed current tends to keep you in the middle. CIRRUS has negotiated this passage several times, and on the last occasion the skipper had a call come through on his ship-to-shore phone, leaving me holding the tiller, so to speak.

Well into the Bay of Fundy, with its tremendous rise and fall of tide, is the busy harbor of Saint John, New Brunswick. When the salmon are running, the gill-netters manning their long, buoyed mesh add to the complications of channel traffic; however, to touch alongside one of their launches and buy one of the catch makes it all worthwhile.

At the entrance to the Saint John River, in the inner harbor, are the famous Reversing Falls, caused by a hard basalt underwater ridge. These are negotiable for about a half an hour at slack water, but even then the conjunction of tide and river current causes great turbulence. Beyond the falls is a wonderful inland cruising area, the great river flanked by hills and farm lands, and navigable for many miles. Diverging from it are the large bodies of water of Kennebecasis Bay, Belleisle Bay, Washademoak Lake and Grand Lake, from the northern end of which a boat of six-foot draft can wind the narrow channel of the Salmon River to Chipman.

In several areas there are long, low grassy islands in the river, and when a large fleet is cruising one may see sails across the land in several directions. Small barns and herds of cattle add interest to the islands. Alluding to the procedure regarding red and black buoys when entering a channel, there is a saying in Saint John River, "You leave the red cows to starboard and the black ones to port."

This area is almost entirely free of our fog friend.

Rendezvous at Pendleton Island. Watercolor, 1972, 14¼" x 20".

The quest of the third Nirvana of inland cruising is by the course far to sea, across the Gulf of Maine to Cape Sable, and down the long coast of Nova Scotia.

Along that shore on the way to friendly Halifax are such thoroughly indigenous ports as Shelburne, Liverpool, Lunenburg and Chester; all busy with the work of the sea. Lunenburg, of course, is the famous building place of fishing schooners, notably of BLUE-NOSE, the last of them to represent Nova Scotia in the fishermen's races against the Gloucestermen sailing the GERTRUDE L. THEBAUD. The tall rigs with auxiliary engines gradually are giving way to power alone.

One year aboard BRENDA, on westerly return from having won our class in the Marblehead-Halifax Race, we set some kind of a record: Lunenburg to Lunenburg in six hours! Having stuck our nose out on a close reach under shortened sail, against a mean southerly wind and sea, our progress was so minuscule and the weather so unabating, that we put back to the welcome lea of the harbor. This tactic provided the opportunity to make the study for the accompanying watercolor, out of the hatchway.

Beyond Halifax are many of the more remote and secluded anchorages: Jeddore, Ship Harbour, Sheet Harbour, Ecum Secum, Liscomb, Whitehead. That there can be good weather, sometimes for days on end, is borne out in the mood of the watercolor *Seaward Channel, Jeddore*. At anchor again is the Alden schooner, GOLDEN HIND, in which we were bound for the Bras d'Or. Skipper George Clowes, a heart surgeon who is an avocational sketcher, was also at

work on this subject with its characteristic little Nova Scotia church in the foreground.

On weathering Cape Canso our ship crosses Chedabucto Bay to Cape Breton Island. Until the latter part of the nineteenth century access to the expansive salt waters of the Bras d'Or Lakes was at the northeast by a deep, narrow arm of the sea, the Great Bras d'Or. The building of the St. Peter's Canal provided entry in the southwest, a boon to commerce and cruising sailors alike.

Yachts in Saint John River. Watercolor, 1960, 17½″ x 29¾″.

Harbor at Lunenburg. Watercolor, 1949, 24″ x 29½″.

Seaward Channel, Jeddore. Watercolor, 1949, 14½″ x 22″.

These wide bodies of water and their long indented arms between the mountains provide extensive
opportunities for exploration by the cruising boat.
Bald eagles are a not uncommon sight; in one arm
called The Boom there are many. As in Saint John
River, the lakes are virtually free of fog—a phenomenon one tries to forget about, knowing he is going to
find some on the long windward haul back to the
westward.

Cape Breton place names are redolent of the
changing and re-changing history of the island, Mic-
mac, French, British and Scottish—Eskasoni, Louis-
bourg, Englishtown, Iona, for example. As I passed
Iona at Grand Narrows only last summer, its significance became greater when I recalled visiting the
Scottish Isle of Mull during the cruise of SHEAR-
WATER two summers before. Iona is also the gate-
way to the Washabuck Peninsula, where many Scots
came when evicted from their crofts by the great pro-
prietors during the infamous "clearances." Neil Mac-
Neil calls it "The Highland Heart in Nova Scotia."

It was at Baddeck, the principal town of the
lakes, that Alexander Graham Bell developed many
of his inventions in communication, flight and other
imaginative fields. A fine museum at Baddeck cele-
brates his ingenuity, while in sight across the water
is his house, Biene Bhreagh, high on a headland.
There, in 1967, an international fleet of cruising
sailors was entertained with a buffet dinner by the
Ladies of the Parish, a bagpipe band, and lads and
lassies in Highland dances. The Gaelic tradition and
tongue are almost more vital on Cape Breton than in
the Hebrides, a land so similar.

Fleet off Baddeck. Watercolor, 1969, 14½″ x 21″.

The host on that occasion was the writer of the foreword of this book. And the paper *Fleet off Baddeck* had its origins on that day.

It never occurred to me while painting these pictures over the course of many years that they bore any relationship one to another; nor that they would sail us off on this unpremeditated cruise to the eastward. Only now do I realize that the whole sail starts, not with a boat, but with a dark mare named Tess, and ends here with another one named Pearl—plain as black and white.

On high meadows overlooking the Great Bras d'Or our friends Guido and Faith Perera own a simple old farm where my wife and I have spent some happy days. Senior resident of this land is a thirty-one-year-old white mare named Pearl, of absolute color contrast to Tess of Naushon. This past summer she could still pull the black buggy over limited distances; and, with the memories of youth mentioned in the introduction, I could not resist making her part of the composition entitled *Pearl*.

It seems he's just an old horse and buggy painter.

Pearl. Watercolor, 1972, 14″ x 21″.

COURSES SOUTH

The Bahamians are great sailors; and for the work boats it is a way of life, in fact of family life. With decks loaded with produce, conches, or with fish in the hold, these able craft from the Out Islands crowd on sail to reach the larger market places, notably Kingston. It is a great sight to be sailing alongside one for a distance, with a subject right there for a considerable time. The watercolor *Island Sloop* was derived from such impressions while cruising in Don Starr's NORTHERN CROWN in 1961, the trade wind sky and bright water a foil for the tawny, patched sails and white hull.

Recently we cruised down the Exuma chain with Bill Dickson in his INCHCAPE, sister to our Maine-based GRAMPUS. We made our E.T.A. (estimated time of arrival) to witness the Out Island Regatta, the races of the work boats at Georgetown, Great Exuma. Anchoring in the cove with the native boats, rather than in the yacht anchorage, we enjoyed the colorful scene, and the aroma of native cooking rising from deck fireplaces, as the graceful boats swung to many poses for the sketchook. As starting times approached, surprising numbers of gaily dressed wives and children would emerge from below decks, bound ashore to watch from Regatta Point, sculled there swiftly in skiffs by the consummate rhythm of tall young boys astand their long oar in the stern.

Island Sloop. Watercolor, 1962, 20½″ x 29″.

The Spice Islands of the Grenadines are marvelous cruising country. In early January 1969, Alan Bemis, Wally Howland, and our wives, chartered VANDA, magnificent old 87-foot ketch of Bob Vaughn-Jones, along with the redoubtable Bob and his Swiss wife Hedy, epicure cook.

We threaded the Grenadines from Prickly Bay on Grenada's south coast north to St. Vincent and back again. Though the brisk trade winds moved us fast, the pace was leisurely from island to island on an average half-day's sail. It was a great sensation to steer VANDA, looking forward to the great bow parting the Caribbean. At one point, with my wife Hennie enthusiastic at the helm, the ketch with mizzen doused covered 14 miles in 1 hour and 14 minutes, or an average of 11.3 knots.

That early in the winter the trades have a lot of north in them. At just the right distance to leeward of the big islands, such as Grenada, you can close-reach northward along the magnificent mountainous coasts in good wind and little sea; but in the passages between islands it is a different proposition. The tides of the Atlantic surge in and out between the islands and are funneled through deep passages. The current effect can be either subtly baffling or stridently obvious, as in Bequia Channel, where with wind against tide the current's edge is defined by bucking white horses of the sea. "Kick 'em Jenny" and the frustrations of passing that rocky islet have long fascinated me. Its name seems to be a corruption of French, "le cay qui me gêne," the cay which frustrates me. There the wind will head you and unseen watery hands will grip the hull and move it sidewise.

Of all the islands, Bequia was our choice, in fact so much so that perhaps we ought to keep quiet about it. It is pronounced "Bequi," and twice we dallied there in the blue-green waters of Admiralty Bay, anchored with the trading schooners.

Admiralty Bay, Bequia. Watercolor, 1969, 14½″ x 21″.

HOLGER DANSKE in the Trades. Watercolor, 1970, 19¼" x 27½".

A Marblehead boat which in only a few years has ranged from the Maritimes to the Baltic or the west coast of Africa is John J. Wilson's HOLGER DANSKE, named after a legendary hero of Denmark, where she was built after designs by K. Aage Nielsen of Boston. John had bought NORTHERN CROWN, referred to in comments about the painting *Island Sloop*, and liked her so much that he asked the same designer to create a larger version, of yawl rather than sloop rig.

In a piece entitled "Flirting with Brenda," Wilson writes entertainingly of his first of four crossings of the Atlantic. This fascinating and informative article derived its title from the experience of anticipating and evading the full force of a hurricane in mid-Atlantic, on a course for the Azores in June 1968. For the return crossing on the southerly route, Nielsen designed a set of twin headsails, a version of a rig much favored for down wind sailing on the high seas. As with ZAVORAH's squaresail, this obviates the frightful slatting and banging and wear, the inadvertent jibes of the normal sails with booms and preventers.

As I write, HOLGER DANSKE is now in mid-passage on her fourth crossing—from Madeira, via Dakar, West Africa. Today, November 17, 1972, "ham" radio operator and blue-water sailor Jock Kiley reports contact with her at Lat. 15° N., Long. 27° 43'W., or about 200 sea miles west of the Cape Verde Islands, making 6½ knots on a course for Barbados. She should look much as she does in the watercolor *Holger Danske in the Trades*, until she is running before one of those black squalls. On these and other phenomena she is making observations for the Massachusetts Institute of Technology in connection with the project FAMOUS—French-American Mid-Ocean Undersea Study, a three-year program of oceanographic vessels and submarines, starting in the summer of 1974.

Headwall, Tuckerman Ravine. Oil, 1970, 28″ x 40″.

PART II

Mountain and Valley: East and West

In the introduction I spoke of my discovery, in 1932, of a new pioneering motif of high snow country and skiing. It was upon this discovery of what could be painted upon climbing those lofty slopes, that it also became apparent that one also had to know how to get down, painting rucksack and all. So, that same year in the Depression, Bill McKennan and I started saving up for a March week at Pinkham Notch. Bill is one of those friends who has gotten me into various kinds of valuable mischief, and is an avocational artist who under different circumstances might have been a professional. He had had a bit of ski experience, and between us we were out to become good at it.

Skis, without steel edges and with not very firm bindings, were relatively primitive then; there were virtually no ski teachers except for Sig Buchmayer and Harold Paumgarten at Pecketts on Sugar Hill, a spot not in our financial orbit. At Pinkham Notch the first ski runs were being cut on Wildcat Mountain; while on Mount Washington was the narrow Fire Trail, for purpose implied, the climbing trail to Tuckerman Ravine and the Summit. It was at the head of this trail, on a brilliant day, that we had our first overpowering view of the headwall of Tuckerman. This is as fine a glacial cirque as I have seen on many a mountain since.

Tuckerman Ravine became to me something like what Mont Sainte-Victoire was to Cézanne; but the parallel stops there! (By coincidence Cézanne's mountain appears, from another angle, in *Midi Sun* in the final section of this book.) Countless times I have made studies in that great bowl; and about once a decade have produced a watercolor or oil, all of them different.

The return to old haunts is evinced in the 1968 watercolor *Massif*, from studies on Wildcat Mountain. This is on a "double elephant" sheet, a paper so large one needs roller skates to lay the washes.

The watercolor is a testament to the cherished alpine land of Mounts Washington, Adams and Jefferson. The afternoon shadow is beginning to envelope Tuckerman and Huntington Ravine. To many skiers and hikers this image will always remain the undisputed domain of Joe Dodge, retired chief hutmaster of the Appalachian Mountain Club chain whose headquarters are down under the valley mist, in Pinkham Notch. "The Mayor of Porky Gulch," master of the guilelessly profane expletive, led many a rescue of sometimes heedless climbers on those peaks so capable of violent mood. In 1932 Joe headed the establishment of the experimental weather station on the summit of Mount Washington which clocked the highest wind velocity ever recorded on the surface of the earth—231 m.p.h., on April 12, 1934. The station has long since become a key outpost of the National Weather Service. It was in these hills that Joe's son Brookie developed into a top international alpine skier.

The drawing of Joe, with the straight face he can keep while making outlandish remarks, was done from life in his house in the Notch in 1938, as part of my series of articles in the Boston Sunday *Herald*. It now hangs in the new Joseph B. Dodge Center for mountain activities in his legendary Porky Gulch, the portrait a gift of the Schussverein Ski Club of which he is a member.

Joseph B. Dodge. Drawing, 1938, 13" x 9".

Massif. Watercolor, 1969, 27½″ x 39″.

My original motivation for painting this 1970 watercolor of farm buildings near Woodstock, Vermont, was that their architecture and setting had fascinated me for a long time, ever since they were *Clinton Gilbert's Farm*. But the painting is significant for me in another way too. On the highway which bypasses the buildings is an historical marker which cites that here in 1934 was constructed the first ski tow in the United States. It was on the hill behind the buildings that Bunny Bertram, a former Dartmouth Ski Team Captain, contrived this rope tow, abetted by Doug Burden, Dave Dodd and Bob Royce. Little did we young tyros, accustomed to herringboning, who rode that recalcitrant rope, realize its far-reaching significance, the eventual evolution resulting in such vast complexes as Vail, Colorado, shown on page 121.

The heavy manila rope has long since vanished, and the smooth snow-cover of Gilbert's Hill glows peacefully in the March sun, marked only by the plumes of a few cross-country skiers.

Clinton Gilbert's Farm. Watercolor, 1971, 14½" x 21".

The sport of skiing has come full circle 'round since that early event in Woodstock, with the renewed and widespread interest in cross-country skiing and high mountain touring.

Much of the skiing this book is talking about is the obverse of The Abominable Snowmobile. Though we all relish the downhill runs at Aspen, Stowe or Zermatt, there is a satisfaction in getting somewhere on your own two feet at a pace that allows one to absorb some wonderful surroundings. This bears a kinship to the rewards of getting somewhere by wind and sail. The journey can be by hill and dale on a pair of light and correctly waxed (one hopes) cross-country skis: or it can be with "sealskins" strapped to the boards on the long climbs to the hut chains of the West and the Alps—to the glaciers and high peaks and the long runs down.

The composite picture *High Mowings in Snow* is of a landscape contiguous to that of the Skyline Trail, a good example of the Elysian Fields attainable by the cross-country skiers. This marked track from East Barnard to South Pomfret has a variation of five or eight miles over wood roads and trails, alternating with open mowings and high ridges, sweeping views and stunning perspectives down over farm buildings. Lacking such terrain one can have a good afternoon on the wood roads and fields of towns much nearer to the cities. As to the alpine tours, more of that later.

High Mowings in Snow. Watercolor, 1967, 20¾″ x 29″.

DESIGN AND DESIGNERS

The architecture of the barns of New England, and elsewhere in this country, often has an integrity and grandeur that makes them true landmarks. With their tall silos, cupolas and gable angles, these structures almost look like castles at a distance.

The one entitled *Triumphant Barn* seems just that, commanding a position on the high meadows above the Mad River Valley, majestic in the light snowstorm. In abstract terms every angle of roof and gable is pleasing, the weathered subtle red of clapboards a foil for the neutrals of the moody landscape. The main ventilation cupola is a masterpiece of design and craftsmanship when studied from close range, with its flaring roof of copper and delicate weathervane. The corn crib too, with its diverging, slatted sides, is a handsome piece.

There was a time, as there was with the coast of Maine, when I took Vermont dairy barns for granted. With changing times and circumstances many of the smaller dairy operations have been closing down, and with this some handsome structures fall into disrepair and eventual collapse.

Triumphant Barn. Watercolor, 1970, 21″ x 29″.

A kind of New England architecture which has always provided a great fascination is that of the trunks and branches of the great sugar maples, those growing singly rather than amongst the many in the sugar bush. I have painted them individually or two or three along stone walls, in every season, with or without their sap buckets.

In company in the sugar bush the trees reach up and do not develop such a powerful anatomy of their lower branches as they do where they have room to spread out without competition. The grooved and craggy bark of the trunk of the rock maple has all sorts of neutral color variations that are subtle and satisfying to paint, especially when accented by the gray-green of the lichen that often grow on the shadow side. The powerful thrust of the branches in different dimensions into the sky has much movement in the subtle play of light, color and direction. In delineating these limbs I sometimes figuratively get caught up there a bit dizzy.

Valued for many reasons, including their use as wood for furniture, these trees contribute heavily to the autumn color spectacle of the Northeast. Their handsome big leaves may be scarlet, orange or brilliant yellow, depending on conditions and season. The two sentinels, *Great Sugar Maples*, were painted above South Woodstock, Vermont, long after their foliage was under the snow.

Great Sugar Maples in Snow. Watercolor, 1962, 14½″ x 21″.

Dr. Bradford Washburn, Director of Boston's Museum of Science, is characterized by an ability to scale the seemingly insurmountable, whether it be a mountain or the establishment of a completely fresh direction for a museum 142 years old.

Upon his return from World War II in 1945, the young director of the New England Museum of Natural History resumed his duties with his sights high. Abetted by board presidents John K. Howard and Dr. Terris Moore, a great mountaineering associate, he wanted to expand the governing society's limited objectives into broader realms of science, and to fashion a teaching museum with many demonstrations and with lively exhibits which the visitors could operate. He also felt that one of its major responsibilities would be to have a large education department focused on the inspiration and development of creativity among children.

In the face of initial skepticism, and after gargantuan efforts by many generous and far-sighted friends over the years, the final major unit of the new Museum, its huge west wing, recently opened at Science Park. Over this span of time, attendance has increased twentyfold and the staff has increased from 8 to over 200!

It was the writer's privilege to be secretary of the Museum's board of trustees for four of the most eventful years in its development, and a board or corporation member ever since.

The drawing of Brad, in three conté chalks and hard pastel, was done from life in 1948, during the most critical phase of the Museum's transition period.

Bradford Washburn. Conté and Pastel Drawing, 1940, 28″ x 22″.

It was executed in early morning sessions, before he started his day's work. A hot spell came and his alpine gear was wilting him. I got out a large life drawing, a red chalk nude, and pinned it to the pull-up shade of the big north window of my Chestnut Street studio. Not surprisingly, Washburn's features instantly resumed their characteristic eager look!

This portrait was executed just after his 1947 Mount McKinley expedition. That expedition spent 89 days on McKinley, climbing both of its peaks and living for over two weeks above 18,000 feet, doing cosmic ray research and surveying for the Office of Naval Research. A companion piece is the portrait of his wife, Barbara, who on that journey became the first woman to reach North America's highest summit, the South Peak (20,320 feet). She is still the only woman to have climbed McKinley's North Peak.

An almost lifetime work has been Brad's unexcelled map of the Mount McKinley area. Published in 1960, it involved a "first" in cartography—that of carrying contour lines visibly through the intricate "cliff drawing." It was the writer's commission to serve as Brad's first intermediary with the world-famous cartographer of Bern and Zurich, for the map was ultimately produced by the Swiss Federal Institute of Topography, and amounts to a work of art as well as science. Washburn's mountain photography, both from the air and on the ground, rated a one-man show at the Museum of Modern Art in New York.

His map of Mount Kennedy, Alaska, followed in 1965, a joint Museum of Science–National Geographic production. His "vacations" are now employed, under the same auspices, in making a large-scale map of the heartland of the Grand Canyon, accompanied by detailed trail descriptions for hikers, botanists and geologists—publication will hopefully come in two or three years.

A glistening curling stone is a handsome object; and when one steps into the shimmering rinks from the early darkness of a northern winter afternoon, the colorful impact of the scene of the game is dazzling.

To one who is only an enthusiastic observer, the nomenclature of this sport, originated possibly in Holland but nurtured by Scotland, is an esoteric dictionary. A basic term, "bonspiel," defines a match between clubs; and though this painting was intended as an artist's reaction to the spirit of the game it does contain elements of technical truth concerning an international match. The stone, sliding toward the concentric rings of the "house," is being persuaded by two of the four members of the "rink" (which also means team) who are "sooping" with their brooms to condition the ice. The stance of the "skip" bespeaks his unquestioned authority, that the stone should stop at the dead center "tee," beneath his broom.

The tempera painting evolved from many sketches made at a country club to which I have long belonged; its identity could be suggested by the primrose and green rings of the "house." The lady patron who acquired this work shortly after its completion said, "Shep, don't you dare ever paint another curling picture!"

Bonspiel. Tempera, 1956, 21½" x 29".

The West Highland cattle, considered to be aboriginal to that part of Scotland, are equally adapted to Vermont. I have seen four herds of these fine beef cattle in various parts of the state, and there are doubtless more.

This composition at Portledge Farm in the highlands of West Windsor was one which absolutely demanded attention, and this it received over parts of several days. The process involved sketchbook studies, direct work with easel, without easel, using the hood of the car for one, or getting into same to warm up or eat lunch. The presence of lunch was sensed by a large and aggressive cat, supposedly hired to take care of the rodents in the barn. Subsequently he was around always, front paws in the watercolor box or climbing my shoulder. He just never wasn't there.

As to the Highland cattle, we quote from a pamphlet of Mr. & Mrs. Harold J. Allbee who then owned Portledge: "... they came prepared. They are fully as hardy as any of the wild animals of New England. With their long hair and thick undercoats, they are equally indifferent to heat, flies and sub-zero temperatures. They don't need pampering or elaborate housing—just a place where they can get hay when pastures are buried in snow. By preference they will calve outdoors, even in snow. Scotties will thrive on rough pastures where other breeds fail to gain, but they will do even better on good pastures."

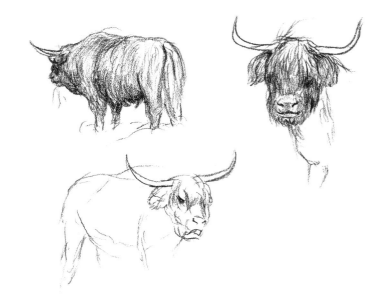

96

Highland Cattle in Snow. Watercolor, 1966, 14½" x 21".

The October sun slants across the clapboards of the white house of Pingree Farm in Massachusetts. The stone building, formerly a stable, offers a contrast in textures. Each building complements the other in the interest of its fine architecture.

New England towns and villages have a heritage of many superb houses and churches, even down to small and simple dwellings. The characteristic story-and-a-half house of the Waldoboro area of Maine, front door with side windows and fan above, is a good example of basic and pleasing integrity of design. For much of this excellent taste the area has to thank Asher Benjamin. His series of books, illustrated by engravings of both design and structural methods, spread know-how to craftsmen of countless country towns. Too often these fine structures have been bracketed by poorly conceived commercialism, which defeats now belated planning. We also have learned to treasure many of the larger houses of the turn of the century, with their mansard roofs, their porches and their porte-cocheres.

Many of the designs of contemporary architects harmonize admirably with meadow and mountain, making good period pieces to go along with their predecessors.

Pingree Farm. Watercolor, 1957, 14½″ x 21″.

Dick Borden, the noted wildlife photographer and conservationist, was for fourteen years president of the Massachusetts Audubon Society, and is inventor of the high-speed telephoto Borden CameraGun.

All of this might not have come about if he were not a good bird shot, as I have portrayed him in 1961 with a favorite pointer, Vim, and if his early business career had not been interrupted by World War II. It was in 1944 that I encountered Dick at Leyte Gulf where he was serving as a lieutenant commander on the staff of Admiral Thomas C. Kincaid's Seventh Fleet, which had just won the great battle of Leyte Gulf. A favorite topic of speculation at that time was what one would go into if the war ever stopped. Borden allowed that he would go into wildlife conservation while practicing with a camera gun he had been developing. He did exactly that, and after a year with the National Audubon Society and two years as executive director of the National Wildlife Foundation, he launched his own enterprise of Borden Productions.

His training in leading a bird enabled him to shoot his heavy, sophisticated, high-frame-speed CameraGun with the very special skill it required. His remarkable slow motion pictures of birds and animals were released in such features as his television series, *Wonders of the Wild*. He also produced much of the footage for Disney's *Vanishing Prairie, Islands of the Sea, Jungle Cat*, and many other nature and sporting features where his high speed gun was a beneficent weapon. His present one shoots at 500 frames a second!

Dick's home is on a pond adjoining the wonderful Great Meadows Wildlife Refuge in Concord, Massachusetts. In this pond he has carried out some interesting researches. Some years ago he successfully introduced the gadwall to the eastern flyways. In spring he obtained wild three- or four-day-old gadwall chicks from Albert H. Hochbaum, director of the Delta Waterfowl Research Station in Manitoba, Canada. These were raised under wire in the pond, and in fall, banded and released. Two such seedings several years apart resulted in the gadwall being established in numbers along the Atlantic Coast. As Borden says, "the young female duckling homes to her natal marsh," and I have seen large flocks of this "dabbling duck" on his pond in autumn.

Richard Borden. Oil, 1960, 40" x 30".

Two areas of Vermont seem to call when the March sun and continuing snow offer conditions for field studies by ski and painting rucksack: the Wood-stock-Pomfret region and that of the Mad River Valley. The conditions, at best, are always marginal for such a sedentary pursuit. Though one might become hot while skiing, after one sits on emptied ruck-sack atop inverted skis for a while, the cold penetrates the person to the extremities, pedal and digital, leaving one incompetent to delineate the compelling subject. By that time the low sun has left the slope; so upon reassembling gear and struggling into ski bindings for a short and usually ineffectual warm-up climb, one makes a macaroni-legged descent to the valley. Some days are beneficent, however, and in the West the high elevation sun is more effective. Whatever their merits, the eventual products have at least the authenticity of such origins.

Mad River Glen has the reputation of being the "skier's ski area," which does not necessarily explain my frequent presence there. Many subjects have been derived from the trails of Stark Mountain, such as *Running the Antelope*. Mad River, similar in terrain to later areas along the main range of the Green Mountains, was exemplary, according to the code established by its president Roland Palmedo, dean of American skiing, in preserving the environmental integrity of the long winding approach up Mad River Glen.

One would think that a painter would run out of subjects, but any year upon return from Waitsfield or Woodstock, I have a notebook full of ideas I didn't get to.

legs are whiter inside
whitish around eyes + muzzle
+ under chin.

Running the Antelope, Mad River. Watercolor, 1970, 21″ x 29″.

One time at a party I met a young lady who exclaimed, "Mr. Shepler, I just love your muriels!"

Before I could adequately respond to the compliment, having no twin daughters by that name, her conversational attention was diverted by a more logical male of her own age group. Thus alone momentarily to ruminate, I realized what she meant and wondered whether she was talking about Annapolis, the Boston Museum of Science, or Williams College.

It could have been Alumni House at Williams she referred to, where I painted five decorative mural panels in architectural spaces designed for the purpose. Three of the four in the West College room had a common reference plane of foreground terra firma; so to be consistent the fourth needed different treatment, for it is set high above a broad door.

From these specifications the fanciful concept of *A Blue Jay's View of Williams* evolved, a composition which could be seen only by such a bird in flight above the Gym Lunch. The diverse elements of architecture of the towers and cupolas of the college, accumulated over nearly two centuries, are in about that relation; but nobody can gainsay the winged draughtsman, for it would take a bit of doing to reach his height of eye.

Towers and Cupolas. Oil, Mural Decoration, 1960, 50″ x 80″.

FAR WEST

After the cruise of the ZAVORAH had concluded at San Pedro in the spring of 1937, I picked up some skis shipped to Washoe Pines Ranch at the base of the Sierra in western Nevada. My friends there had concluded I must be lost at sea, for the skis had arrived months before.

Some painting sessions followed in the still-deep snows of the high Sierra at Donner Pass, which then was innocent of ski lifts, as well as at the ghost town of Virginia City, famed in Mark Twain's writings.

The next destination was Banff, Alberta, to meet Bob Notman for some climbs and glacier touring with Swiss guide Eddie Feuz. The value of the snow craft and local knowledge of an experienced guide was borne out in a climb of Mount Victoria. The approach is up the lower Victoria glacier to a great mountain wall atop which is the hanging upper Victoria glacier. Feuz predicted that when the sun reached it a big section of ice would avalanche. We climbed at right angles to a shoulder, and upon returning there from the summit, down the knife ridge, we heard a tremendous roar below us. At the little stone hut on the shoulder we brewed some tea and waited, Eddie estimating the time when the hanging glacier would have hardened up. When we retraced our course below it, the big crevasses were completely buried in astronomical tons of pulverized ice and snow.

The watercolor illustrated is from a less ticklish area north of Banff, *Bow Glacier, Bow Peak.*

Eddie Feuz. Drawing, 1937, 8″ x 10½″.

Bow Glacier, Bow Peak. Watercolor, 1937, 14½″ x 21″.

Otto Lang. Drawing, 1938, 7½" x 5".

The following March, 1938, architect Walford Walden and I stuck our skis in the rumble seat of my 1934 Ford roadster, and set forth for Berthoud Pass, Colorado, and the Pacific Northwest on the pretext of getting the hang of painting the high snow country.

The watercolor *Ski Runners of Mount Baker* derives from episodes there and at Mount Rainier. Before the short climb of Table Mountain to work on this picture, I alerted my friends as to exactly where I would be. When I was ready to descend, the sun was off the slope and the trap crust had formed on the spring snow, so cautious flat traverses and kick turns ensued. While making one of these stationary turns I caught a tip in the crust and spilled, knocking off my light metal rimmed spectacles. With snowy eyeballs, I made a grab for the spectacles but saw them taking off straight down the fall-line of the steep slope. Being somewhat myopic I lost sight of them, but could hear them tinkling along the glaze and finally stop—but I couldn't be sure. More traverses across the line of descent led, finally, to their retrieval. They had not, after all, slid all the way to the front door of Mount Baker Lodge to alarm the watch.

It was in that year that Austrian Otto Lang, now a noted motion picture producer, formed a branch of the Arlberg Ski School on these slopes.

Ski Runners of Mount Baker. Watercolor, 1938, 14″ x 21″.

Big Cottonwood Canyon and Little Cottonwood Canyon are wedged in between some very high mountains of the Wasatch Range of Utah. The heads of these defiles are way up at 8,000 feet or so, and one starts up from there to ski, to paint, or to do both at once.

Compatriot Standish Backus and I were doing just that: Early one spring morning we stuck sealskins to waxed skis, shouldered painting rucksacks and started off in the general direction of Up, from Brighton in Big Cottonwood. The day was dazzlingly good, and we were in quest of subject matter with no preconceptions. We stopped briefly to sketch a great gnarled tree growing out of a cliff, but the vast snow bowl between peaks, above us, beckoned us on. At the crest of the bowl is a lofty saddle known as Albion Pass, and we were curious about the next raspberry patch beyond it. All the time we climbed we watched a golden eagle sporting in the updrafts of the steep bowl and peaks. At the crest of the Albion saddle the spectacular world of Alta lay before us. A section of the crest's snow cornice had broken away, offering a safe studio facility right there.

Stan has a way of audibly criticising himself while working, but a hoarse whisper beside me made me look up to see the golden eagle a ski length above our heads, his imperious yellow eye as surprised as ours. His sportive flight had just grazed the snow of the saddle. Upon recovering his composure the eagle would have witnessed something resembling the watercolor *On Albion Pass, Alta.*

On Albion Pass, Alta. Watercolor, 1951, 14½″ x 21½″.

The country around Aspen, Colorado, offers a wealth of subject matter, and I have produced several paintings there. The watercolor *Return from Star Basin* is a depiction of the less familiar, bagged in the remote high hinterland. Possibly that is why I used it, because it played so hard to get.

Up a long canyon, accessible by car, and beyond Mt. Hayden, is the relic of the tiny mining town of Ashcroft. From there it is a long but not very steep climb up to a varied ski touring area centered on the Lindley Hut, named after Al Lindley, Olympic skier of 1936. Lindley had taken a leading interest in such ski-touring facilities in this very area, when he was killed in the crash of a private plane. The first time I was at Lindley Hut it was just opened but not complete, and one of Al's young sons was there working on it.

Like spokes in a wheel, from the hub of the hut, are access routes to four huge, high basins: Cooper, Star, Pearl and Montezuma. I have puffed up to this area three times: once with film-makers John and Lois Jay and twice with Henry Stein and other Aspenites. On two of these occasions our stay was truncated by weather which found John Jay challenging at chess on his tiny magnetic board. Prognostications of continuing storm or resultant avalanche danger made it futile to stay; but on the third occasion Star Basin, Pearl Basin and Pearl Peak rewarded our persistence with some thrilling climbs and runs.

Return from Star Basin. Watercolor, 1960, 14¾″ x 20½″.

One of the real rewards of snow-mountaineering painting is in having the company of another artist with the same interest. Two people in particular of this sort are Standish Backus and Florian Hammerle; with one or the other or both, I have had some marvelous expeditions.

I initially encountered Stan—who comes from Santa Barbara, California—at Pinkham Notch in 1936, when he was looking over my shoulder at a flub of a watercolor I was doing. All this led to later joint operations in the West, particularly around Sun Valley. When Sun Valley started in 1936 I designed the first poster for this fine venture of Averell Harriman's Union Pacific Railroad, and over the succeeding years other posters and work for reproduction.

Life at Sun Valley had then, and still has, a brilliance, warmth and joy. Both in the valley and in the distant hinterland there was a great variety of subject, and when we were not playing hooky running the lifts, our skis took us in many painting directions. While we were there with our wives in March 1941, Stan was called to active duty in the Naval Reserve, and that was that. He was so valued by his command later on, that pleas and pressures exerted by us other Combat Artists did not effect his transfer to that duty till nearly VJ-Day. During the Geophysical Year he went back on active duty as official Navy artist for Operation Deepfreeze in Antarctica.

The large watercolor *New Snow on Baldy* belongs to Lois and John Jay; he is the renowned raconteur of ski films. On the eastern horizon are the tall peaks of the Pioneer Range, to which this yarn next takes us.

New Snow on Baldy. Watercolor, 1950, 21″ x 29″.

When the Union Pacific built Sun Valley it also constructed two cabins for spring ski touring in the alpine worlds of Owl Creek and Pioneer. The latter is just in the lee of a high saddle, facing the head of a deep canyon and the towering peaks of the Pioneer Range. It is a two-room affair, and fittingly enough the double deck bunks are provided with Pullman curtains.

I have gone there several times with Florian Hammerle, sometimes joined by Stan Backus, Dick Durrance and others, grinding up the three-hour ascent with heavy packs of provisions. Florian, usually known as "Flokey," was then a ski teacher at Sun Valley, and our trips were after the closing of the school. He had been trained as a designer in Munich, and paints well and with concentrated gusto. He was thorough in his snow craft, a master at anticipating the potential avalanche, a matter which has to be borne constantly in mind in this sort of endeavor; on his other side he was a natural clown, a constant source of merriment.

One spring the two of us got snowed in by a cyclonic snowstorm, which after two or three days displayed its sunny center, then gave us the other half. For refrigeration our meat was bundled up and hung to the shadow side of the eaves, and each night this attracted the attention of a beautiful and bold pine marten who couldn't quite figure a way to get the prize; but as the cabin became more deeply buried his chances grew better. Florian's years in this country had not much improved his English. At night I awoke to see him rushing out into the storm half-clad, shouting, "Dot Gott dam martyr!"

Snow Squalls at Pioneer. Watercolor, 1951, 21½" x 29½".

The Basques from the Pyrenees seemingly have the temperament and background to tolerate the isolation of working flocks of sheep north through the ranges of the West with the progress of spring. Known here as "Basquos," the company, lone on a great landscape, is always moving to behold. Their encampments are of course always near water, their saddle and draft horses usually tethered, their wagons at angles, with the cook wagon reminiscent of the Conestogas of the pioneers. The flock surrounds the scene with the small herding dogs taking their ease, but keeping an eye on the situation. Historically, in their native mountains the Basques also used Great Pyrenees (of which we raised two generations in Massachusetts), as guard dogs against predatory wild animals. So far I have not heard the deep, welcoming bark of one so engaged in the West.

The sighting of the Basquos is cause to drop everything else and get out the sketchbook. Once I came upon them near a water hole, the whole assemblage reflected in the surface, against a high range in the distance; another time dwarfed in the great canyon of Senate Creek. It was upon just reaching Sun Valley from a climb to Pioneer Cabin with Florian Hammerle, the valley in snowless spring, that I saw a flock coming along a ridge bordering Trail Creek. Skis and gear, except for a sketchbook, were quickly stowed, and I hastened back up the Trail Creek dirt road, following the wagons. Much of the day was left, and from it came the drawing *Basquos of Trail Creek*. It may be of interest to the layman that we reproduce both the drawing and the resultant painting, to illustrate an approach. The sketch was reinforced by considerable written notes on color,

mood, this and that, and supported by the visual memory which becomes acute with training. One's own sketches, however fragmentary or frightened, as were mine in World War II, are of more value to the artist than any other source.

Basquos of Trail Creek. Watercolor, 1951, 14″ x 21″.

On the Lodgepole, Vail. Watercolor, 1972, 10½″ x 14½″.

Painting in the high snow country has always been a severe strain on my character. When the weather is good for painting, it is usually even better for skiing. Maybe that's why I have sought out distant slopes where there isn't the temptation provided by the lucky people whizzing by.

There was great temptation last February at Vail, Colorado, for two reasons. The first was that my old mountain-painting ally Stan Backus had to cancel a long-laid plan to join us there; and the rest of the party was the Dick Prouty family who were skiing like mad all of the time. The second explanation was that Vail sells "Grandpa Tickets"—half price for age 65 or over! With all those wonderful runs such as Riva Ridge and the Bowls it is positively wasting one's money not to ski. So I didn't get very far afield, that time.

However, the watercolor *On the Lodgepole* shows that something was accomplished—and one can still ski after lunch.

PART III

The Interminable Cruise

Lieutenant Commander Griffith Bailey Coale, USNR, had been a mural painter of note in civilian life. In September 1941 he was called on active duty, an event which was brought to the attention of Admiral Arthur J. Hepburn, former Commander-in-Chief of the Fleet, who was then Chief of United States Navy Information. Hepburn had the imaginative idea of finding what an artist could accomplish with our destroyers on the North Atlantic Patrol, the convoy duty of the "undeclared war." Of such an experiment I knew nothing whatever.

When Pearl Harbor happened, and we were besieged in two oceans, I felt unjustified in going on with my painting, and obtained a commission as a lieutenant (jg.) in the Navy. I was deployed to an intensive sea-duty course at the Midshipmen's School at Northwestern University. It seems that while I was there "learning how to Navy" Commander Coale had returned from the North Atlantic and Iceland with some impressive material. He had been in the action of the torpedoing of the destroyer U.S.S. REUBEN JAMES, and had recorded significant scenes in Argentia, Newfoundland, and Iceland. His book *North Atlantic Patrol* was a well received sequel to this effort.

Coale's fine job apparently put Admiral Hepburn and Commander E. John Long to thinking. Long, an Annapolis graduate, had been brought back on duty from his work with the National Geographic

to head up all matters pictorial for the press. These two officers, along with Coale, started a search for professional artists in the Navy who were also sea-duty qualified deck officers—a basic requirement. Though I did not know Griff Coale, he apparently knew my work through the Arthur H. Harlow Gallery in New York, where he discovered that I was in the Navy. He wrote me a letter asking if I would be interested in orders to a new Combat Art Section. Having sworn off for the duration, I could hardly believe this, and my answer naturally was affirmative. The time came when the school course was finishing and we all were getting our orders. Mine were to a ship, but an hour later a second dispatch set came, cancelling the first and ordering me to report to the Combat Art Section in Washington. To coordinate this infant program the Navy had brought on duty the deputy-director of the Corcoran Gallery of Art, Lieutenant Commander Robert L. Parsons.

As I look back over my shoulder at those years, I feel an inexpressible sadness, an uncertainty as to whether my work accomplished what it might have, but a tremendous pride in the naval service and its men, as I came to know it.

I was the second tyro artist to be sent out, and Bob Parsons got me a set of orders to Admiral Halsey's South Pacific Force that made Flag Secretaries gape when I handed them over, with the bright light glaring on my stripe and a half. The orders were broad, wide-ranging and quite autonomous. The implication was that I was supposed to be where the action was, and should be so informed.

My first duty in getting to my destination from the West Coast was on the destroyer CRAVEN,

Air Defense, Battle of Santa Cruz. Watercolor, 1942, 21″ x 29″.

where I began to learn the duties of junior officer-of-the-deck. Aboard the U.S.S. SAN JUAN, colorful anti-aircraft cruiser of the fleet's fastest Atlanta Class, we partook in the Battle of the Santa Cruz, October 26, 1942, an aspect of the battle for Guadalcanal, the third great air-sea action of the Pacific. After Coral Sea and Midway, with new construction not on hand, the only two operational aircraft carriers were HORNET and ENTERPRISE of our Task Force 16 under Admiral Kincaid. We were the only barrier to the Japanese having the sea wide open to Australia. In this action HORNET and PORTER were sunk, ENTERPRISE heavily damaged, and others including SAN JUAN to varying degrees. It was a victory in the sense that the badly hurt enemy retired, but shattered Task Force 16 could not have mounted another air attack. It was in this action that famed "Battleship X," the new U.S.S. SOUTH DAKOTA, so distinguished herself as an anti-aircraft vessel, as we saw her in the watercolor *Air Defense*.

Duty with the beleaguered First Marine Division on Guadalcanal was followed by that on other ships, and transfer to U.S. Naval Forces in Europe for the year preceding the Normandy Invasion.

This section on the war is only to illustrate a few of the more important episodes, out of many paintings and drawings which I executed during three and a half years.

Air Contact, North Atlantic was actually all painted in rough seas aboard U.S.S. CHAMPLIN during an important troop convoy. If you keep your drawing board part of yourself, it's surprising what you can do.

The Battle for Fox Green Beach is a big oil which evolved in stages from drawings made from the bridge of the destroyer U.S.S. EMMONS, on D-Day, in the intervals of a job of target identification. EMMONS and DOYLE had accompanied minesweepers sweeping beach approaches during the night. Returning with the early morning attack EMMONS had her forefoot practically aground as she closed in to bombard and to give fire support to the troops pinned to the shingle above the shoreline. Fox Green was the bitterest sector of the Normandy Invasion, and was a frightful battle.

Even in such stiuations the Navy kept its irrepressible humor. Late on D-Day EMMONS was deployed to the outer screen because of ratio of ammunition expended. It just happened that the executive officer was an old skiing friend, Lieutenant Commander Eugene M. Foss, USNR, and as we steamed along we sighted another skiing friend's ship, the fleet minesweeper RAVEN, commanded by Lieutenant Commander John F. Madden, busy sweeping. Skipper Billingsley suggested that we send a blinker signal, the old ski teacher's exhortation, "Bend zee knees!" RAVEN's bridge promptly blinked back, "I bend zee knees when they stop knocking."

PT boat squadrons 21 and 27 were under command of H. Stillman Taylor, whom I had known of as skippering his family's yawl BARUNA, winning Bermuda Races. The PTs were the first U.S. vessels into Manila Bay and the macabre scene of Manila Harbor. In *PTs and Paratroopers* we were in support of the 503rd Paratroop Regiment's landing on Corregidor, a feat which later-captured Japanese documents estimated to be impossible.

Air Contact, North Atlantic. Watercolor, 1943, 14″ x 21″.

The battle for Fox Green Beach, Normandy. Oil, 1944, 34″ x 44″.

PTs and Paratroopers, Corregidor. Watercolor, 1945, 21″ x 29″.

The phenomenon of living under the inhuman threat of Kamikaze attack for months on end is something hard to describe. Possibly the watercolor of a close one on HORNET, successor to that carrier sunk at Santa Cruz, may have the feeling. That was in the spring of 1945 off Japan, and it was only then that the Navy revealed the existence of the suicide squads: there was a logical reason, for dead men tell no tales of their success or failure. However, this tactic had been going on for months, particularly in the early part of the Philippines campaign. In Destroyer Squadron Five operating around Leyte, we lost half the squadron, sunk or badly damaged in a few weeks. As one of the Kamikaze just missed the bridge of flagship FLUSSER, we could see the expression on the goggled pilot's face as he flashed by to explode in the water in a great flash of bomb and gasoline. The calm reaction of armored-force General Sir Herbert Lumsden, aboard as Churchill's observer, was: "Oh, he funked it, he funked it! He didn't have the nerve." This gallant opponent of Rommel on the Libyan Desert was killed a few weeks later in Lingayen Gulf when a Kamikaze hit the bridge of the NEW MEXICO.

As I observed in the preface, "Finding the Azimuth," my directions have been influenced by some people I haven't known. I have sometimes wondered about those vectors on which Griff Coale's initiative deployed me.

Following V-J Day the Naval Academy at Annapolis commissioned a mural project for Bancroft Hall. For this I redesigned *Air Defense* to a thirty-foot long lunette in the main rotunda, and the Normandy and Corregidor subjects to a pair, each twenty feet long, in the midshipmen's mess. Griff Coale, whose field this was, painted two panels of the attack on Pearl Harbor and night action off Guadalcanal. Bill Draper designed a trio about the invasion of Guam.

Fighter Pilot in Ready Room
U.S.S. Hornet   Dwight Shepler USNR
1945

Kamikaze. Watercolor, 1945, 21″ x 29″.

ADOPTED LANDS

Otto Furrer of Zermatt was a Swiss guide, and in the mid-thirties both F.I.S. world ski champion and winner of the Arlberg Kandahar. Quadrilingual and much travelled in the Alps, he was warmly greeted everywhere he went. It was an irony as well as a great loss that he was killed on his own home mountain, the Matterhorn as seen here in *Winter Hay, Zermatt*, a peak which he had climbed well over a hundred times, when a fixed cable on the Italian side broke loose. The accompanying drawing of Otto, in three conté chalks, was done in Zermatt.

With his expertise on skis and his wide knowledge of mountains, Otto was good company for ski touring expeditions. He guided Ted Bremer, my wife and me on several ascents from the hut chains of the Ortler region of the Italian Tyrol, in 1939. We had been in the hinterland for quite a while when Otto encountered another guide just up from the valleys who informed him that Hitler had marched into Prague. Otto was sure in his own mind that the Axis was going to war, and decided that as Swiss and Americans we had better get out of Italy and Austria, back to Switzerland.

It was a few days later that we met again in his native Zermatt, where we went on a short tour with some spirited friends of his from Geneva who called me "Roosevelt." After this, Otto and I set forth on a hut circuit of several days, with some ski ascents which included that of Monte Rosa from Bettempshutte at 9,200 feet. This resulted in the greatest downhill run I have ever had. We started off in the darkness before the April dawn, for the long climb to Signalkuppe which is just short of 15,000 feet, the frozen crust hard

Otto Furrer. Conté and pastel drawing, 1939, 14″ x 20″.

under our skis. Otto's early start had timed things just right, for after the short final rock climb to lunch at the little iron hut overlooking Italy, we hit the descending stages of snow at just the right phase of softening as we flew down the Grenzgletscher.

The illustration *Castor and Pollux* is a 10 x 14 inch watercolor which I painted near Bettempshutte at that time.

You packed most of your own food to such high huts, and after the climb over Theodul Pass (which you had to make then) we sailed down the lower flank of the Matterhorn on the long run to Cervina, Italy, visions of a big meal in mind. As we entered a fine little inn Otto looked positively fierce with his deep bronze and impressive stubble; while after a bath and shave he looked conversely boyish. The tail-coated waiter proffered the dinner of the evening in a silver casserole. Lifting the cover Otto revealed, "Last night chicken, night before chicken, nothing but chicken!"

Winter Hay, Zermatt. Watercolor, 1955, 28¾″ x 21½″.

Castor and Pollux. Watercolor, 1939, 10″ x 14½″.

FERDINAND AND ISABELLA

It was while I was working in 1965 on two different architectural pieces, one in Spain and one in Portugal, that the far-reaching influences of the Spanish monarchs, Ferdinand and Isabella, repeatedly came to mind.

A most fascinating motif in perspective, color, form and general atmosphere is a great staircase mounting the heart of the Alfama, in Lisbon. This old section flanking the east side of the center of the city survived the great earthquake of 1755. At the foot of steep, narrow lanes and steps lies the mouth of the River Tagus, while from these heights one would have seen Columbus sail forth with his three ships on the voyage commissioned by these imperious and quixotic monarchs. The impact of their reign upon both Europe and the New World is something to reflect upon, particularly if after the day at work you relax to hear the marvelously haunting melodies of the Fado singers at some café by the waterfront. Lisbon and the Tagus is also the arrival and departure point of many transatlantic cruising boats. It is no reflection on the seamanship of the skippers of such vessels as HOLGER DANSKE, twice calling here, that the course to the Indies under sail was earlier clarified by the mariner from Genoa.

Alfama Steps, Lisbon. Watercolor, 1965, 14½″ x 21″.

In February 1965 there was a sign at the main entrance of Hospital Real in Granada, Spain:

Ministerio de Educacion Nacional
Direccion General de Bellas Artes
Conservacion de Monumentos de la 7a Zona
OBRAS DE RESTAURACION

It took no great linguist to understand the message, so I entered through a great iron-studded door, half ajar, into this huge masonry building constructed as a hospital under the direction of Ferdinand and Isabella. Its Renaissance design is in four multi-storied quadrangles, topped by a tower of ecclesiastical mien. The structure was unoccupied, and I wandered unhindered through various levels to look down into the cloistered courtyards, encountering only isolated knots of masons and other workmen who took my curious presence for granted.

It was to the great entrance hall that I kept returning. The scene reminded me of Muirhead Bone's masterpiece in etching, *The Dismantling of St. James Hall,* though the process going on was the reverse in this instance. The Spanish craftsmen, working on dizzying and spindly-legged scaffolds, restoring carving, plaster and wood, were in fascinating combinations of perspective. Their equipment was mainly the basic one of human muscle. For two days the great doors were pushed full open for the illumination of the morning sun as I worked in a dank corner till the fingers would do no more. One could almost see the monarchs striding in on a visit, those who lie in their tombs in the Royal Chapel of the nearby Cathedral.

In full sight outside those doors, over the Alhambra, were the Sierra Nevada where people were skiing, and there were donkeys in the snow.

Restoration of Hospital Real, Granada. Drawing, 1965, 13″ x 10″.

Above Château d'Oex. Oil, 1958, 24″ x 30″.

The oil winter landscape *Above Chateau d'Oex* is the theme of another Swiss episode. Down in the valley below is the village of that name, the center of le Pays d'en Haut, the high country of the Canton of Vaud. The sight of this painting, borrowed from my college roommate for reproduction, makes me homesick.

It was here in 1954–55 that we and our three children lived for a full year in a fine little old chalet, just above the center of the town. Our girls, twelve and fourteen, were in a French-speaking local collège. With one exception they were the only non-Swiss; starting Latin in French is quite a gambit. Our son, aged eight, was in an entirely private school, but enjoyed the run of the village; in this dairy valley, center of Gruyère cheese production, you could rely on the local people to keep an eye on all children rampant. During that fifteen months in Europe we rented our home in Massachusetts, and I painted for over a year without trying to sell anything.

Harriet Hubbard, widow of Charlie Hubbard of ZAVORAH and the Arctic, spoken of earlier, was living there with her three young children. Through her we met many interesting and hospitable townspeople. Amongst these were two painters, John Paschoud and François Masson; we became great friends and working companions. John, Swiss-English, was a combination of architect, artist and landscape gardner. François, in his late twenties, was an ebullient former ski champion; and as most artists must, he had other strings to his bow. In winter he was the top ski teacher in the École Suisse de Ski, and more recently its director. François hadn't taken a fall all season till one day when, as we were coming down Schönried, he was unhorsed from behind by a human rocket from Bern. He then demonstrated his lingual skills in Swiss-German, French and English, in rapid succession. In summer François was a tennis pro on the local courts. In spring and fall he painted intensively.

So it was in the fall of 1954 that the three of us set forth in my "Plymoot" station wagon for Provence. This is an area where I have worked on three different occasions, and which is in my blood; but in this company that trip was the best. François knew Provence thoroughly, and in fact now owns an old *maas*, or farm, in the Vaucluse. We painted furiously every day, finally collapsing at some sidewalk café for some of the *rosé du pays*. Most of the time the mistral, that high wind off the Massif Central, was blowing out of a brilliant sky. We all had combinations of those wonderfully-made painting-box easels by Julien of Paris. John and François, who were working in oil with canvases upright, sometimes hung rocks to their three-legged rig; working flat in water-color I found my board departing a couple of times.

Of the many out-of-the-way places known to François was the village of Fuveau on a colline south of Cézanne's Mont Sainte-Victoire, which appears as a ridge in the background of *Midi Sun, Fuveau*. Though everything else on that expedition was in watercolor, this one was actually developed from a drawing, bringing to bear the vivid experiences with the Provençal light.

Midi Sun, Fuveau. Watercolor, 1955, 21½″ x 29½″.

During that year, *en famille* we criss-crossed France in several directions, as well as Switzerland and parts of Italy, but not on the fly. For quite a time we based at the little Hôtel de France on the harbor of the small Brittany port of Audierne, while I painted in the general environs. The houses, the atmosphere and the people are very reminiscent of Cornwall, the Northwest Coast of Ireland and the West Highlands Coast of Scotland, even to the bagpipes at the fêtes. *Breton Houses, Cornouaille*, with the kelp stacked to compost, is to me characteristic of that coast. It was right near there one day that all five of us took a crack at the same composition in various media. All of these works are preserved in my collection.

Everywhere we went we found the French *sympathique* to an itinerant family armed with butterfly nets and transporting jars of pupating moths, overripe conches and other mollusks. After I paid our bill at the Hôtel de France the proprietress observed the denominations of the poster-like franc notes projecting from my U.S. size wallet. She would not let me go on with what she considered inadequate finance, even though within two or three hours we would be at Dinard where the Banque de France was a correspondent on my letter of credit. She insisted that I take some back and send it by postal money order from Dinard. As we drove off, the entire staff, chef included, were out to wave us adieu.

François Masson. Drawing, 13″ x 10″.

THE OUTER HEBRIDES

Transatlantic yawl SHEARWATER made this port on the north side of Dublin Bay in a full gale at four o'clock in the morning, forty-eight hours out of Helford River, Cornwall. This 47-foot Ted Hood "racing machine" showed both her windward capabilities and seaworthiness as she beat around the Lizard and Land's End, and as a dramatic sunset illuminated Longships Light, reached off for Ireland while the wind faired and increased. Such modern spade rudder designs can be cranky to steer down wind, but fast!

Her basic crew was the salt-encrusted Clowes family, who had sailed her from Quisset, Massachusetts, in 1969: skipper Dr. George and wife Peggy; medical student Alex; Tommie, now Coast Guard Lieutenant (jg.); and daughter Edie, college student. Others joined for parts of the voyage to Norway. My wife and I, who have sailed with this blue-water outfit for twenty-five years, were signed on for the first thousand-plus miles of this marvelous experience, departing from the Solent.

The little Port of Howth as shown in the watercolor, excludes the ire of the Irish sea behind impressive breakwaters and moles. Within, the warm-hearted Irish yachtsmen, who knew the vessel from the previous summer's international cruise of the southwest coast, rolled out a green carpet. We searched out the Book of Kells, and dined in great company at the Abbey Tavern at Howth, where balladeers followed the rhythm of a remarkable gent who played a pair of beat-up spoons on his knee.

Inevitable departure fix was from Ireland's Eye, the small island just off Howth. The course was for the Northwest Channel, the 18-mile-wide pass between Ireland and the Mull of Kintyre in Scotland. When I was on destroyer duty either night or weather had shrouded that headland, but now shafts of sunlight played dramatically upon it as SHEARWATER sped into the Sound of Jura and on to the Western Isles. We threaded our way through those majestic mountainous islands, through the kyles and sounds and sea lochs, circumnavigating Mull in the process to visit ancient Iona.

During a two-week period just before this, along the West Highland shore, we had witnessed wonderful warm, sunny weather, and had looked out over these same waters ruffled to 10 to 15 knot sailing breezes. Now the weather saw us coming, evidently, and produced a series of storm systems from the Atlantic, between or during which we sailed. As we hove into the little harbor of Canna, the wind which we had been anticipating was crowding 55 knots.

Arriving under sail seems to open up an entrée, a hospitality which one might not otherwise enjoy. Our big anchor held at the little island of Canna, but it was not until the next day that the gale had lessened enough to get a boat ashore. The first person to greet us was the genial botanist and writer, John Lorne Campbell, Laird of Canna, who offered us tea, scotch, and baths. It was astonishing to find that his wife was the Margaret Shaw who had written an old *National Geographic* article we had been reading aboard. The article dealt with the Gaelic songs of the Outer Hebrides, which she had recorded by written word and music note over a period of several years.

At the Isle of Rhum, operated entirely by the Nature Conservancy, director Peter Wormell offered

Breton Houses, Cornouaille. Watercolor, 1956, 20½″ x 29″.

Port of Howth, Ireland. Watercolor, 1970, 14½″ x 21½″.

every facility, and later, when invited aboard with his wife and two children, told much of great interest. It was, however, at Castlebay on the outer island of Barra, that I found the most endearing acquaintance. Hennie and I were ashore sketching; the ruddy-cheeked and strong-faced elderly woman was at the head of the path to a house in the foreground, carrying two milk cans. She greeted us and asked us to stop in for tea later. It proved to be a charming visit in a house built by her grandfather, the first slate-roofed house on the island. Her name was Morag Macaulay.

In the consequent painting, *Morag's House, Castlebay*, she is depicted beside her house, as SHEARWATER's tall rig rounds Kismul Castle out the harbor mouth to shape a course across the broad Minch to the distant Isle of Skye.

Morag's House, Castlebay. Watercolor, 1970, 21″ x 29″.

The Dog Watch

This book is witness to many horizons, both tranquil and perilous. There were those hundreds of dawns and dusks when that rim of the ocean either appeared or faded from sight during General Quarters at battle stations—that long hour when attack, particularly by submarines, is most likely. Those were hours of haunting memory, the often splendid visual orchestration of sea and sky accompanied by the sounds of the combatant ship—the commands to the helm, the talker reporting all stations manned and ready, "fire one, fire two," the sepulchral "pong" of the sonar beating its hollow rhythm. It became so that one wondered whether he ever had, or ever again would be entitled to view the sky and sea without considering the threat of the enemy they might conceal.

However, such a day did come. With some practice it became possible to view the sun's course with equanimity, and this reality became an unbelievable privilege. For the sailor to cope with the sea alone seems a quite adequate pursuit, and for the ski trooper, the glacier or the mountain. The dawn watch, aloft in the shrouds, has only to avoid a premature landfall on some low-lying atoll, not to attack it, or in the historic Jeffrey's Ledge Race to locate that lone and unlighted whistling buoy called 2JL, hooting to itself out there on the dark ocean. The ski tourer, climbing on the hard pre-dawn crust of the Alps watches the high skyline reveal itself, no longer manned by gunners.

Such experiences seem to heighten appreciation of the finer works of nature and of man, and I now am glad that I painted them when the opportunities came.

Credits

The paintings and drawings comprising this selection of the artist's work were most generously lent for reproduction from the collections of the following:

Mr. and Mrs. Alan C. Bemis
Mr. and Mrs. Richard Borden
Mr. and Mrs. Francis A. Brewer, Jr.
Mr. and Mrs. Alexander H. Bright
Mr. and Mrs. William L. Butcher, Jr.
Mr. and Mrs. Paul C. Cabot
Mr. and Mrs. Hadley C. Case
Dr. and Mrs. Edwin F. Cave
Mr. and Mrs. Roger J. Clapp
Mrs. Paul Collins
Mr. and Mrs. Bigelow Crocker, Jr.
Mr. Michael R. Deland
Mr. and Mrs. James T. Dennison
Dr. and Mrs. Robert M. Donahue
U.S.S. ENTERPRISE VIII
Mrs. I. Garrett Forbes
Mr. and Mrs. Frederick W. Griffin
Mrs. Seavey Griffith
Mr. and Mrs. Waldo H. Holcombe
Mr. and Mrs. John C. Jay
Mr. and Mrs. David Jeffries

Mr. and Mrs. Howland B. Jones, Jr.
Mr. and Mrs. Robert M. P. Kennard
Mr. and Mrs. Caleb Loring
Mr. and Mrs. James L. Madden
Mr. and Mrs. Willard R. May
Vice Adm. and Mrs. John L. McCrea
Mr. David S. McElwain
Mr. and Mrs. John R. McLane, Jr.
Dr. and Mrs. James S. Murphy
Mr. and Mrs. Joseph T. Nicholson
Mr. and Mrs. Guido R. Perera
Mr. and Mrs. Arthur Perry, Jr.
Mr. Maynard W. Powning
Mr. and Mrs. Richard Prouty
Mrs. George Putnam
Mr. and Mrs. George Putnam, Jr.
Mr. and Mrs. Laurance S. Rockefeller
Mrs. M. Ducey Ryerson
St. Botolph Club of Boston
Mr. and Mrs. William H. Sawyer III
Mr. and Mrs. A. Thorndike, Jr.
Mr. and Mrs. Robert Truesdale
United States Navy Combat Art Collection
Mr. Samuel Wiley Wakeman
Mrs. Bradford Washburn
Mr. and Mrs. David P. Wheatland
Williams College
Mr. and Mrs. John J. Wilson

The painter's works are in many additional private collections, as well as in these permanent collections:

Borough Museum, Dartmouth, England
Hospital for Women, Boston, Massachusetts
Museum of Fine Arts, Boston, Massachusetts
Browne and Nichols School, Cambridge, Massachusetts
Brooks School, North Andover, Massachusetts
Children's Medical Center, Boston, Massachusetts
Museum of Art, De Pauw University, Greencastle, Indiana
Dwight D. Eisenhower Museum, Abilene, Kansas
Emerson College, Boston, Massachusetts
Harvard University, Cambridge, Massachusetts
Leland-Stanford University, Stanford, California
Museum of Science, Boston Massachusetts
Osage Indian Museum, Pawhuska, Oklahoma
Massachusetts General Hospital, Boston, Massachusetts
United States Naval Academy, Annapolis, Maryland
Unitarian-Universalist Association, Boston, Massachusetts
University of Alaska, Fairbanks, Alaska
University of Maine, Orono, Maine
Wentworth Institute, Boston, Massachusetts

AN ARTIST'S HORIZONS

was composed in Baskerville type by P & M Typesetting Company, printed by The Meriden Gravure Company, and bound by Robert Burlen & Son, Inc. Designed by Raymond M. Grimaila.

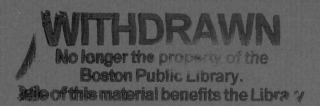